How to Be Miserable and Alone

HOW TO BE
MISERABLE
AND
ALONE

(OR DISCOVER A LIFE THAT TRULY MATTERS)

KAISER JOHNSON

Our Sunday Visitor
Huntington, Indiana

26 25 24 23 22 21   2 3 4 5 6 7 8 9

Our Sunday Visitor Publishing Division
Our Sunday Visitor, Inc.
200 Noll Plaza
Huntington, IN 46750
1-800-348-2440

ISBN: 978-1-68192-645-2 (Inventory No. T2502)
1. RELIGION—Christian Living—Spiritual Growth.
2. RELIGION—Christian Living—Social Issues.
3. RELIGION—Christianity—Catholic.

eISBN: 978-1-68192-646-9
LCCN: 2020950263

Cover and interior design: Lindsey Riesen
Cover art: Adobe Stock

PRINTED IN THE UNITED STATES OF AMERICA

*To my grandmother Vera, who taught me about God,
and to my wife, Keeley, who shows me the love of God.*

Contents

Prologue

Twelve Simple Tricks To Be Miserable and Alone!

(How the advice we take from our culture is ruining our lives)

Everywhere you look you're assailed with advice on fixing your dead-end career, your shabby body, and your subpar sex life, whether or not you knew you were suffering from these shortcomings. But how could you not know, when you're reminded by every magazine in the grocery store, every blog post, every popular Instagram account, every Facebook share, every online and social media ad minutely tailored to know and exploit the point where your interests and anxieties meet?

Every minute of the day, we're told to feel a great lack in our lives as they are, and that the only improvement to be found comes in the perspective du jour. The problem is that this perspective is a schizophrenic one, divorced from consistency, let alone truth. For instance, consider these contradictory visions:

- Happiness lies in a perfect body ... but also, we should promote body positivity and end fat-shaming.
- Marriage is so important and essential to human rights that it's wrong to deny it to the LGBTQI (etc.) community ... but also, marriage is an outdated institution that we should really just move past.
- There is no all-powerful Being who has a personal investment in our lives and hears our prayers ... but there is an all-knowing universe that, while impersonal, makes our dreams come true if we dream hard enough.
- #timesup for men who use women ... but using someone sexually is empowering, and slut-shaming needs to go.
- Gender-reveal parties are the best and worth spending hundreds of dollars on ... but also, gender is just a social construct and it's wrong to impose that on anyone.
- Babies are amazing and cute, and a pregnant royal or Kardashian-Jenner or Perry or Queen Bey is to die for ... but also abortion is an innate right, and humans should stop reproducing because the world is over-populated.

I'm sure you can add more bullet points just from a quick social media scroll. But perhaps these contradictions show that maybe, just maybe, our culture doesn't have all the answers, and we need to look elsewhere if we're to find happiness, empowerment, rights, and dreams worth fulfilling.

There was a really popular plot device in a lot of '90s romance films (and in plenty of other stories throughout the years), where everything was going perfectly for the young lovers ... until a rival showed up. The rival knew both the guy and the girl, and wanted the girl for himself. So he would reveal (or make up) something damaging about the guy and tell the girl, who would accept it without question and suffer no explanations from the guy, and frequently find love in the arms of the rival instead. The thing that I always found so unbelievable in all of this was that *everybody knew* that the rival was a lying, manipulative jerk. The girl had no precedent to believe anything he said, had many reasons instead to trust her love, and yet would listen to the rival. Whether it's *I'll be Home for Christmas* or *She's All That* or *Ten Things I Hate About You* (though there it was a female rival), the point is, she suddenly has this bizarre trust in someone who she knows doesn't have her own best interest at heart. I've always thought that was so crazy and stupid … and yet I've done it too! I spent years listening to the counsel of a world and a culture that — if I had taken two seconds to think — I could have easily seen didn't have my best interest in mind.

By the time I got to college, I had all these burning questions about life, love, sex, being a man, and doing the right thing — and the world's answers just plain weren't working (more about this later). A lot of my friends felt the same way. Maybe you've felt it as well. But then, through the surprising grace of God, I started hanging out with some really good Catholics. When we talked about life, love, sex, being a man, etc., I discovered that they had answers too … only their answers were inspiring. Not just inspiring! They were beautiful, they challenged me, and far from the contradictory words of wisdom I was hearing from the world, they made sense together as one whole. The more I heard and learned and put into practice, the more I realized why they all clicked. Every single question I could come up with each had the same answer: the Incarnation of God. Jesus Christ and his Mystical Body, the Church, are the answer to every question we could possibly conceive. However, for many of us, Catholics included, it's one place we forget to look.

We see this search for meaning and connection everywhere in the world around us: from self-help books promising to answer our questions, to magazine and clickbait articles calling out to solve our problems, to dating apps, porn, and a hookup culture trying to fill the emptiness in our hearts ... an emptiness that, it turns out, only God can fill. You see, our story isn't a story just of our search for truth; it's the story of Truth searching for us. It's the story of the God of the universe desiring to reach us so much that he becomes one of us. And if we allow him to be one with us, he won't just answer our analytical questions: He will give meaning to our suffering; he will provide hope in our despair; he will draw trust out of our uncertainty; he will create connection where we feel alone.

It's so easy to forget Christ is knocking at our hearts. I've experienced fear with my own plans for my life, heartbreak and suffering in a divorce and annulment, regret for my many mistakes. But I've also experienced hope, gratitude, joy, and new life every time I let go, trust in God, and let him be in control. We often unconsciously assume that the Church is stuck somehow in the past, and couldn't have answers to the questions of our day, or we fear that we'll be judged and given a long list of "thou shalt nots" instead of answers that heal our hearts. Nothing, however, could be further from the truth. The fact that the God of eternity took on human nature tells us that the Gospel is good news for all mankind, whether in first century Palestine or twenty-first century America, and that it's not a bunch of "nos," but good news of great joy.

In this time of your life, what questions are you asking? What are you struggling with? Where do you need new solutions? Do you want to be miserable and alone? Because I've got twelve simple tricks (that I have unfortunately tested) for you to try! Or do you want to discover just how great your life can be? If so, read a little further.

1

The Universe Has a Plan!

(Searching for the Meaning of Life)

"Tarot cards, like astrology, are a mystical way to form a deeper connection between yourself and the universe — and also not a bad party trick."

— *Cosmopolitan*, "Your Tarot-Reading Primer"[1]

"You perceive it in the depths of your heart: all that is good on earth, all professional success, even the human love that you dream of, can never fully satisfy your deepest and most intimate desires. Only an encounter with Jesus can give full meaning to your lives."

— Pope Saint John Paul II, "We Wish to See Jesus" (homily)

---

[1] Sami Main, "Your Tarot-Reading Primer," *Cosmopolitan*, June 12, 2020, https://www.cosmopolitan.com/lifestyle/a27334893/how-to-read-tarot-cards/.

What's the purpose of life? Does it have meaning? Or perhaps the more pressing question we each ask ourselves: Does *my* life have meaning? How do I make my life meaningful? Ask a hundred people their thoughts on these questions, and you may hear a hundred different answers. The fact is, these are questions that all of us think about, and perhaps one of the reasons we tend to be so frightened of death is because one corollary of "Does my life have meaning?" seems to be "What if I die and my life didn't mean anything?"

Most people have some kind of answer to these questions — magazines, talk show hosts, and self-help books certainly do — but most of them are the wrong answers. Honestly, much of the time it feels like we're just looking for comfort. "Life's about having stuff and feeling good" — can you tell I live in California? — or, "Life's about having friends and family. ... My friends *are* my life," or, "Life's about success, however you define it!" Or how about, "Just know the universe has a plan!" On that note, do you know anybody who doesn't believe in a personal, loving God, who cares about their life and has a purpose for it? I do believe in God, and even so, sometimes I can empathize with that feeling of being abandoned by God ... that maybe he's not there, or just doesn't care. But does that friend not believe in God, and yet believe that the completely impersonal universe has a grand design for his or her personal life? I have a harder time understanding that. There's another answer to the question of life that might sound good, but in reality is devoid of any useful sentiment: "Life has whatever meaning you give it." What does that even mean? And how is it supposed to help me?

Now don't worry, I'm not going to respond with something stupid like, "The right answer is in the right question," or, "Let me answer this question with another question." No, there is an actual, real answer to this question of our hearts, and it's one that satisfies. But first let's dive a little further into why none of the answers above satisfy. The problem here is twofold: First, we're equating the purpose or meaning of life with *having* purpose and meaning in life. Second, all these answers actually assert that life in itself is meaningless, and it's only the extrinsic stuff that gives life meaning. Let's tackle the second part first.

If life is about circumstantial qualities, we're in trouble; whether those circumstantial things are tangible (like cars or houses or money), or intangible (love, happiness, familial accord). In the case of tangibles, it seems clear that just having them doesn't give life meaning. If it did, we wouldn't hear of rich, successful, famous people struggling with addictions, committing abuse, overdosing, or killing themselves. These are the problems of people who are failing to find meaning, not those who experience an abundance of it. Even if we add intangibles into the equation, we don't really get closer to a satisfying answer. You see, if life is only about friends and family, or happiness or success, what does it mean if you are permanently deprived of those things? Say, for instance, you lose everything you have: your stuff, your comfort, your job, your family, your friends; and golly, you're trying hard to be happy, but that feeling goes away too. Does your life still have meaning in and of itself? That's one of the questions a guy named Job asked while morosely scratching his sores with a broken piece of pottery, sitting on a hill of garbage after all his stuff was destroyed, and his kids died and his wife all but abandoned him. The Book of Job is worth reading from beginning to end, but if I were to try to boil it down to the essential bits, it would probably look like this:

Job: God, what did I do to deserve this? How is it fair that you gave me all that just to take it all away? Why don't you just kill me instead?

God: Who made Leviathan?

Job: OK, fair point.

That's my summary, but the actual book is much better. Job begins his experience by saying, "The LORD gave, and the LORD has taken away; blessed be the name of the LORD." And then after worsening circumstances finally drive him to complain and question God, God's response (essentially that he creates and does things far beyond our ability to comprehend), though enigmatic, satisfies Job, who says:

> "I know that you can do all things,
>   and that no purpose of yours can be thwarted.
> 'Who is this that hides counsel without knowledge?'
> Therefore I have uttered what I did not understand,
>   things too wonderful for me, which I did not know.
> 'Hear, and I will speak;
>   I will question you, and you declare to me.'
> I had heard of you by the hearing of the ear,
>   but now my eye sees you;
> therefore I despise myself,
>   and repent in dust and ashes." (Jb 42:2–6)

There is something in God's response to Job that challenges him, that makes him ask himself a new question: If God told me the meaning of all of this, could I even understand it? In his *Introduction to the Book of Job*, G. K. Chesterton writes, "He has been told nothing, but he feels the terrible and tingling atmosphere of something which is too good to be told. The refusal of God to explain His design is itself a burning hint of His design. The riddles of God are more satisfying than the solutions of man." He goes on to point out that Job, this "best man in the worst fortune," prefigures another who is to come; another whose response to wounds and ills and spite will not be to question God, but simply to say, "Not as I will, but as you will" (Mt 26:39). To further quote Chesterton, in the short story *The Sins of Prince Saradine*, Father Brown says, "We here are on the wrong side of the tapestry ... The things that happen here do not seem to mean anything; they mean something somewhere else. Somewhere else retribution will come on the real offender. Here it often seems to fall on the wrong person."

Why do I bring up all those quotes and verses one after the other? Because they drive to one central point: While the individual occurrences of life — those extrinsic circumstances, blessings or deprivations — might escape our understanding, they don't need to deprive us of the knowledge of our own life's meaning ... exactly because they aren't what provide the meaning of our lives. Job asks, "How can my life have meaning if you take away all these things from me?" And God's reply essentially is, "Because the meaning of your life is not found in any of those things." To give another example, when the Jews are in exile in the Book of Jeremiah, they ask, "Should we even be getting married or having kids with the world the way it is right now? Should we build houses when they'll really belong to our oppressors? How can our lives have meaning when nothing is our own and everything's so up in the air?" But God reassures his people that, even if they don't understand what's happening, they can still trust him because all those "things" they're worrying about don't define their lives. "For I know the plans I have for you, says the LORD, plans for welfare and not for evil, to give you a future and a hope. Then you will call upon me and come and pray to me, and I will hear you. You will seek me and find me; when you seek me with all your heart, I will be found by you, says the LORD" (Jer 29:11–14). The meaning of their lives is found in their relationship with God, not in externals.

This brings us to the other part of the problem: the meaning *of* life vs. having meaning *in* life. Let me put it another way.

Lots of people ask, "What's the meaning of life?" Or "Why are we here?" That's still a general existential question (though an important one!). But most of us care a lot more about another question: "Why am I here? Do *I* really matter?" Let's take the general existential meaning-of-life question first. Since becoming Catholic and learning the answer to this, it's kind of baffled me how many people, even how many Catholics (including those with formal theological backgrounds) can act like it's an unanswered or unanswerable question. Have you ever asked about the meaning of life, and been disappointed with the answer you received? Or have you not really ever stopped and asked the question? Or have you heard an answer that is inspiring and ought to be life-changing, but realized that you rarely let it change your life? This last one is me most of the time.

Really, we've had the answer for a long time: "God put us in the world to know, to love, and to serve him, and so to come to paradise" (*CCC* 1721). When it comes down to it, our own experience tells us we all want to be happy, whether or not we're quite sure how to go about it. Our reason can tell us (and Scripture does a pretty darn good job corroborating it) that if we all have that desire, and God made us, that it's a desire he must have placed in our hearts. And if it's a desire less of body than of soul, then it's one that no earthly thing can satisfy. That's why Saints Peter and Matthew talk about true happiness in terms of *beatitude*: intimate knowledge and unity with God, becoming sharers in the divine nature (cf. 2 Pt 1:4 and Mt 5:3–12).

Why are we here? For true, deep, intimate relationship with God. Does my life have meaning? Yes! Whether I'm rich or poor, sick or healthy, successful or thwarted, get a bunch of stuff or lose a bunch of stuff, live that #billionairelife or not, my life always has meaning and always has purpose. God made me because he loves me ... which is a crazy thing to think about. How does God create me out of love for me? I'll go with Job on this one, and say that while I may not understand, that's perhaps because the truth is too wonderful to understand. There's an analogy in the love of parents for their children: I think it was Venerable Archbishop Fulton Sheen (but try as I might, I haven't been able to source the quote, so if I'm quoting you or a friend of yours, let me know) who said that the love of husband and wife is so great, that in nine months they give it a name. In other words, true love is incarnational; it's so great that it *must* create. Knowing that God created us out of love helps us understand the meaning of our lives and perceive our place in the world.

My life, not just human life in general, but *my* life, *me*, *I* was created in the image and likeness of God. And so were you. "So God created man in his own image, in the image of God he created him; male and female he created them" (Gn 1:27). Interestingly enough, knowing this helps me understand my purpose! If God created me in his image, and God is love (cf. 1 Jn 4:8), then I'm called to love as God loves. I'm here on this earth to love God with all my heart, soul, mind, and strength, and to love my neighbor as myself (Mk 12:30). As Saint Augustine put it in his *Confessions*, "You have made us for yourself, O Lord, and our hearts are restless until they rest in you."

Unlike all the suggestions for the meaning of life that we might have been told, this answer stands entirely independent from external circumstances, tangible or intangible. No matter your circumstances, you are capable of fulfilling your purpose in life and living a life full of meaning. And that's perhaps an important clarification to make so we can move from finding the purpose and meaning *of* life to finding meaning and purpose *in* life: You can always live out this call because love is an *action*, not just an emotion. "Like" is an emotion, "affection" is a feeling, but real love is an action. In the *Summa Theologica*, Saint Thomas Aquinas says, "To love is to will the good of another." This understanding does us the great favor of moving love from the territory of fleeting emotion into the realm of practical process. How do I love my neighbor, my family, or my enemies? I will their good, and perform the actions of love. To put it maybe a little over-simply:

- If I spend quality time with my wife and my daughter, I am loving them. If I don't, I'm not.
- If I speak words of kindness and counsel to my friends, and perhaps even more importantly, to my enemies, I am loving them. If I don't, I'm not.
- If I honor my father and mother and thank them for the gift of my life, I am loving them. If I don't, I'm not.
- If I give of my time, talent, and resources to those who need it, I am loving them. If I don't, I'm not.

The same holds true with our relationships with God.

- Do I pray, and just spend time with God? If I do, I'm loving him, and if I don't, I'm not.
- Do I honor God with my decisions and use the talents he has given me to glorify him? If I do, I'm loving him, and if I don't, I'm not.
- Do I give thanks to God for everything, the things I understand and the things beyond my understanding, the things that go my way and those that don't? If I do, I'm loving him, and if I don't, I'm not.

I said a second ago that this way of looking at love does us a great favor of making love a practical question. It also does us another great favor: It takes a ton of pressure off of us. Personally, I can frequently fall into the habit of looking at my life and decisions as though one right decision will set my life on the correct path, will cement the meaning and legacy of my life. On the flip side, if I get something wrong, make a mistake, I've permanently missed my once-and-for-all opportunity to fulfill my purpose, as if I had one shot and I threw it away. The good news for me (and for you, if you've ever had shades of these thoughts or feelings) is that I'm totally wrong. When we understand our purpose as knowing, loving, and serving God, and loving our neighbor as ourselves, and we understand that love is an action, that means we have a thousand opportunities daily to fulfill our purpose! Do you feel like you're not living your best life? Then instead of beating yourself up, dragging yourself down, or having a quarter- mid- or late-life crisis, check in and refocus on loving God and loving those around you.

Does "knowing and loving God" sound too esoteric? Then make it practical. Someone (I forget who) once told me that we come to know and love someone best not by talking to them, but by listening to them, by hearing their words and appreciating their actions. So in addition to the active ways of love suggested above, what about sitting with the words of God and listening? Pick a passage of Scripture, something short, maybe one verse of the Beatitudes or another instance of Jesus teaching, sit in silence for five minutes, maybe even ten or fifteen minutes, and let God speak those words to you. And then do it the next day. And again the next. We'll get into this more later, but while God is always speaking to us, we tend to hear him best when we set time aside in silence to listen.

"OK, I get all that, but what about this feeling I've always had that my talents, passions, and hopes are all for a purpose? That those all have meaning?" Fair question, and one that again moves from the existential to the specific. I think most of us can relate to the feeling that we have these desires in our hearts or these talents we've been given that we want to exercise and live out, and that doing so will bring us joy, satisfaction, and meaning. That might mean anything from having natural artistic talents and a desire to express them, to a passion and aptitude for service, to a head for numbers, to a longing just to learn and understand. The list goes on in as many ways as there are people, because we really and truly are made different and unique by a God who loves us. It's true, God really did give us gifts and desires that he intends for us to use and grow, as Jesus points out in the parable of the talents in Matthew 25:14–30. So how do we deal with this part of the process of living? The big answer is to understand that it's a process. In an online video series I cohost, called *Catholic Central* (it's on YouTube), we have an episode called "Purpose and Meaning of Life" that deals specifically with this aspect of the question. I'm credited as the writer of that episode, but I can't take credit for the great outline of discernment that the theology team at Family Theater Productions put together for the episode. They break down this discernment of the use of our gifts and talents in this way:

1. First and foremost, we're called to "develop and deepen our relationship with God." We need to spend time in prayer, with the sacraments, growing close to God so we have ears to hear his voice.
2. Secondly, we "look at our lives and experiences." We get introspective and ask God and ourselves what desires he has put in our hearts, what talents he has given us, and in what moments we have felt the most fulfillment.
3. Third, we "explore the possibilities." As you understand better your desires, your talents, and the small ways in which you've found fulfillment, are there states of life (single, married, religious life) and avocations (jobs, careers, even hobbies) that those point to? What are the ways of living out love and

service for God and neighbor that all these things might work together to serve?

4. Fourth, we "talk with others." Just as you are called to love your neighbor as yourself, so are all your neighbors! Find people close to you whom you can trust, and let them also live out their vocation to love by giving you counsel and pointing out things you might not have thought of. Then bring those to prayer too, which happens to be step five …

5. "Pray for wisdom and perspective," so that in all things you return to God and better understand the ways in which he calls you personally to love him and those around you, and in so doing, live out your purpose in life.

And again, remember that God made you out of love and for this purpose of love. This is who you are in your very core. This is the meaning of your life. You can't mess it up, miss your opportunity, or waste your life, just so long as you always come back to God and let your restless heart find rest in him.

SO NOW WHAT?

- If the *Universe* has a plan, great, you're good, no need to do anything or seek truth or whatever. The Universe has got your back! So, what can you do to just chill out today?

- But if *God* has given your life both purpose and meaning, how can you fulfill that today? Pick two practical, actionable things (even small ones); one to grow in relationship with God, and one to live out love of neighbor. Will you sit in silence with Scripture? Reach out and tell someone who doesn't expect it that you love them? Go to Mass even though you'd rather sleep a little longer? Do the dishes when it's not "your turn?" What ideas can you come up with to put love into action and fulfill your purpose today?

2
Do What You Want!

(Why self-fulfillment is making us miserable)

*"Get clear on your vision, make your plan, take
action, reassess and then revise. Never fails."*

— Entrepreneur Magazine, "16 Actions to
Take to Achieve Any Goal"[1]

*"Our concern must be to know God's will. We must enter
that path: if God wants, when God wants, how God wants."*

— St. Gianna Molla

---

[1] Deep Patel, "16 Actions to Take to Achieve Any Goal," *Entrepreneur Magazine*, 27 August, 2018, https://www.entrepreneur.com/article/318347.

I recently read a book on success and productivity called *The 10X Rule*, by Grant Cardone. It's an interesting book, and there's a lot of good in it, but one part in particular stuck out to me. Cardone says that the major limiting factor on his own success, and consequently his own happiness, has been not thinking big enough. He meets his goals, and then wishes he'd picked bigger ones. This makes me think of the Norman Vincent Peale quote, "Shoot for the moon. If you miss it, you will still land among the stars," and the poem excerpt by Erin Hanson that launched a thousand memes, "And you ask 'What if I fall?' / Oh but my darling, / What if you fly?"

Now, maybe you love both those quotes, but I think Cardone, Peale, and Hanson are all stopping short of a major realization here. Peale suggests setting big goals, and finding satisfaction even if you don't achieve them. Erin Hanson seems to suggest fearlessness in seeking fulfillment. And as with Cardone's writing, there is good to be gleaned here, both in the value of courage and of discovering enjoyment of the "not half bad!" But while I find good in all three ideas, even if I occasionally roll my eyes at the pastel sentimentality, Cardone unconsciously clues us in to a startling truth: Self-fulfillment isn't fulfilling. Time and again he has shot for the moon, hit it, and his only response is, "OK, what's next?" He's fallen, he's flown, and isn't impressed by the view. He concludes that it's the striving and achieving that we like;s it's the winning that we enjoy far more than the possession of what we've won. So pick bigger goals than you ever think possible. If you achieve them, maybe they'll be big enough to make you happy; and if you don't, maybe you'll be even happier, because you never had the chance to be disappointed that getting what you wanted didn't make you happy.

This leads us to yet another quote: "For what does it profit a man, to gain the world and forfeit his life?" (Mk 8:36) I wonder if those two clauses are more connected than we generally perceive. Is there a direct connection between gaining the world and losing your soul? Can you gain the world *without* losing your soul? Or do you only try to gain the world because you are losing your soul? Do we hope that if we can just gain the world, we might finally satisfy our souls? Let me run through a little review of my own experience, and tell me if you can relate.

Here are a few life goals that I've had over the course of my last decade of existence:

- I want a yellow Jeep Wrangler.
- I want to work as a series regular on quality network, cable, and streaming television shows for the rest of my life.
- I want a great, loving marriage.
- I want to have enough money that I never have another moment of anxiety about finances.
- I want to own a home ... just kidding. I want to own several homes, one of which is situated on my own private island.
- I want a tiki adventure bar in my home at which I can host parties, and also, like, just have a great bartender at all times for when I just want a cocktail and don't want to make it myself. You know, just a live-in, on-staff bartender at my beck and call, like all healthy, normal people want.
- I want to go to heaven.

Now that I've probably given you more insight than you ever wanted into my shoot-for-the-moon dreams and wants, let me break down a little bit how my life actually has gone and tell you how I feel about it.

- I have a Jeep! It's not a yellow Wrangler, but it's a

Jeep and I can drive it over bumpy terrain! I never do though, and any time anyone compliments it, I knee-jerk explain that it's not really the one I want.

- In addition to having starred in a top box office film (*Unplanned*), I have worked on great quality network, cable, and streaming television. Not as a series regular though, so naturally none of that counts.

- I have a great, loving marriage, better than I ever could have imagined (especially after my previous long-term relationship — more on that in a later chapter). We communicate, support each other, love each other, and have the best baby daughter in the world. And yet, so often, I find myself realizing I'm not engaged in what's going on with us: I let the TV, my phone, the stuff I "have to do" distract me from just loving and appreciating this dream come true.

- I'm making easily two to three times the money I was a few years ago, but I manage to increase my expenses and tastes and spending to still feel anxious.

- OK, we still rent, but we have very much made our house a home, and yet I still act as though we are in transition. "Yeah, this is fine, I guess … for now."

- I hand-built a tiki bar with two of my friends for my patio, and the entire inside of the house is covered in adventure-themed decor (which my wife has been kind enough to fall in love with out of love for me). But I only tend to appreciate it when someone else visits and goes, "Oh wow, that's cool!" or "Wow, that's weird," or "Huh … tell me the story behind all of *this*." Otherwise, I barely even notice that I'm basically living in The Jungle Cruise ride, which is *my dream of dreams*.

As for heaven, let me illustrate where I'm at on that with a little story from Thomas à Kempis out of the *Imitation of Christ*. A guy is anxious, wavering between hope and fear, and he goes to a church to pray.

While meditating on these things, he said: "Oh if I but knew whether I should persevere to the end!" Instantly he heard within the divine answer: "If you knew this, what would you do? Do now what you would do then and you will be quite secure." Immediately consoled and comforted, he resigned himself to the divine will and the anxious uncertainty ceased. His curiosity no longer sought to know what the future held for him, and he tried instead to find the perfect, the acceptable will of God in the beginning and end of every good work.

Ninety-nine percent of the time I'm this guy before he hears the divine answer. If I want heaven, I should be showing up to a relationship with God right now! But I keep saying, "Just let me take care of all this stuff I've gotta do, God, then we can hang out. I'll see you on Sunday for an hour, though, let's catch up then!"

Let's review. All the things I want, to the degree I've attained them, don't satisfy me. Even those things that excited me before I had them (my first network booking; being on my favorite TV show, "Stranger Things;" having a tiki adventure house), pretty quickly stop being stimulating, or only prompt me to react "OK, what next?" And I seem to be letting all these things distract me from what *does* satisfy me when I really put it first: my relationship with God and my family. In the times I've been most connected to God, and when I am really present with my wife and daughter, I'm incredibly satisfied! I have none of the "OK, what next?" response. I think of moments I've had of just sitting in adoration, no specific prayers or agenda on my mind other than simply to be there with God, and peace fills me. When our phones are off and my wife and I are just doing anything together, whether it's washing dishes or having a date night, I'm into it, and I love it. I'm not thinking about what comes next; I'm too busy appreciating her presence and our time together. The same holds true with moments with my daughter. I remember G. K. Chesterton's great quote on motherhood from his book *What's Wrong with the World*: "Babies need not to be taught a trade, but to be introduced to a world. ... How can it be a large career to tell other people's children about the Rule of Three, and a small career to tell one's own children about the universe? How can it be broad to be the same thing to everyone, and narrow to be everything to someone?" While he applied this to the greatness of motherhood, I experience the same as a father. When I sit with my daughter and do the things she's excited about, I'm reintroduced to this wonderful, magical universe anew along with her.

These relationships in my life that bring me such joy and satisfaction? *None* of them have gone according to my plan! The relationship I was in before, which led to my first wedding (again, more on this later) — I knew what I wanted, and I was determined to make it go to plan. But it blew up in my face. The woman I'm now blessed to call my wife showed up at a time I didn't expect, under circumstances I never would have guessed. On paper, we didn't even seem to be a good match. But she and I agreed to see if there were greater plans at work than our own, and I can't thank God enough that we did and that he delivered. When it came to children, I wanted to have a son first, because wouldn't that be best? And yes, in writing this down I am deeply aware how absurd all the correlated assumptions I apparently possessed must have been, since never having had any experience of fatherhood, I still believed I knew exactly how it should go. Thankfully my plans there were inconsequential, God didn't consult me, and our daughter is the light of my life. And the more I look in retrospect at my relationship with God, the more I see that my plans don't seem to do it any favors. You see, I tend to put my relationship with God as one aspect of my life, instead of letting it fill my life and give me life. By contrast, when I show up, spend time with Christ in the sacraments, and invite him to be present throughout my life, I'm always surprised by how much happier I end up.

Can you relate to any of this? What have you set out to achieve, successfully achieved, and then thought, "What's next?" or now today say, "Yeah, OK, that's something I did." What desires have you fulfilled, only to find that they're not fulfilling you? If you like, take some time to sit down and write out goals you've had that you've accomplished and things you've wanted that you've got. Write out goals you still have, and the "why" behind them. What will they do for you, how will they change your life? Now go through all of it, meditate on everything you've written, and write a little more. How do you feel about it? What realizations or thoughts are you having? Where do you find fulfillment and where don't you? Do any of your thoughts surprise you? If you're anything like me, you might find that the actual fulfilling things in your life aren't those items that would go on a self-fulfillment list. You might take a second here and thank God for the things that do fulfill you. Now, I'm not saying we should scrap all our goals, skip school, not go to work, so that we can just spend time with family and God. I am saying we should second-guess the worldly wisdom that says, "If you can discipline yourself and fulfill your goals, you'll be fulfilled!" Now, I *am* in favor of discipline, and I *do* believe that Grant Cardone isn't satisfied because his goals aren't big enough. However, I've come to the conclusion that the only goals big enough to satisfy won't be his goals at all, or mine for that matter. Maybe, just maybe, we'd be better served not by picking our own goals for our lives, but by assenting to God's goals for our lives. After all, "For as the heavens are higher than the earth, so are my ways higher than your ways and my thoughts than your thoughts" (Is 55:9). If we're looking to find some bigger goals, it sounds like God has some ready for us, ones we can't necessarily think up on our own. "For I know the plans I have for you, says the LORD, plans for welfare and not for evil, to give you a future and a hope" (Jer 29:11). Perhaps we shouldn't be shooting for the moon or the stars at all, but heaven itself. Perhaps Grant Cardone is more right than he knows, and only the goals written in eternity truly have the ability to inspire and the capacity to satisfy.

So what does that mean for you and for me? Well, if we want goals and dreams and desires that satisfy, we should show up and do the work to discover the deeper goals, dreams, and desires that God has placed on our hearts. How? The five steps for discernment of purpose from the last chapter are a great place to start. I would especially emphasize steps one, two, and five, where we pray, get introspective, and pray some more. If we're hoping to get a clue into God's goals for our lives, so to speak, developing a relationship with God and being present with him is the only way to set that foundation. Self-examining to better understand who we are in that relationship gives us insight into where we're at in this moment.

If you're craving a more specific framework, as I usually do, for how to implement this introspection and prayer in a daily, ongoing way, the Examen of Saint Ignatius of Loyola provides a pretty great outline. He asked all his community to do the Examen twice daily, once at noontime (a "lunch examen," if you will) and once before going to sleep at night. At Loyola Press' IgnatianSpirituality.com, they summarize the process of the Examen like this:

1. Become aware of God's presence.
2. Review the day with gratitude.
3. Pay attention to your emotions.
4. Choose one feature of the day and pray from it.

5.   Look toward tomorrow.[2]

Essentially, find a quiet place where you can be calm and con-templation is possible. Let yourself know that God is there with you. Think about your day (or your day so far, if it's a lunchtime examen), and highlight at least a moment or two that you are grateful to God for, or can be grateful to God for if you haven't been yet! Look at the things, people, and events in your day that brought you peace and that you brought peace to, and those that didn't, and how those moments affected you (or more accurately said, how you let them affect you). Whether you pick a blessing, a joy, a suffering or a challenge, pick one feature of the day, and pray to God with it. No need for a ton of words, just lift it up to God and listen. Close out by bringing this awareness, this dia-logue, and this understanding forward to the next day, so that you can perceive more as blessings, your sufferings can be less-ened, and your response to each thing and every moment can be more virtuous tomorrow.

Now, you may not immediately judge that you're getting a lot out of this. You may not be sitting there listening and suddenly hear God speaking to you like, "Hey Kaiser, check this out, here's a sweet idea for you." I certainly haven't. I think I've maybe really heard God speaking to me twice in my life, and it was nothing like that, despite my judgment that it would be really convenient for God to just hand me a syllabus for my life rather than rely on this whole prayer thing. But that's kind of the point. If God is love, and I'm made in the image of love, then my purpose in life, my goals and desires, will be found in relationship — and first and foremost in my relationship with God. So then, don't be discouraged if you don't get a lot out of it at first. You and I didn't

---

[2] If you want a little more detailed breakdown, BustedHalo made a great infographic of the Examen: https://bustedhalo.com/summer-school/summer-school-june-29.

know what we wanted to be when we grew up the day we were born (I went from police officer to food critic to architect and somehow ended up here at actor, God help me). We didn't develop the strongest relationships in our lives, or any relationship in our lives, overnight, and we can't expect speed in a relationship with God or in a proper discernment process either. But if you show up, get quiet, become aware of the presence of God, and spend time in gratitude and silence, those plans-higher-than-yours will begin to come clear to you, and in the stillness you will hear the voice of God (cf. 1 Kgs 19:11–13).

To close out the chapter the way we started, I'd like to appeal to another too-oft-memed quote (in my opinion). You may have heard, or seen mawkishly illustrated, the saying, "If you want to hear God laugh, tell Him your plans." I'd like to think that the sentence that follows should be, "But if you want to be happy, ask him to tell you his."

SO NOW WHAT?

- Are you unfulfilled right now? Well, Entrepreneur magazine says that if you get clear on your vision, make your plan, take action, reassess and then revise, it never fails. Need I say more?
- If you'd like to get clear on God's vision and goals for your life, do two things. Start with the fulfillment exercise above (you know, the "write out goals you've had and achieved, and things you've wanted and now got," bit) and meditate on that for a while. Step two, begin doing a daily examen. If you're spending silent time with God per the last chapter, take a few minutes in that time to examine your day, express gratitude, and prayerfully consider tomorrow, or the rest of the day.

3

Be Yourself, Love Yourself!

(How we've started settling for ourselves at our worst)

"However bad you are, it's crucial to accept yourself the way you are. Loving yourself is a must if you want to live a successful and happy life."

— Womenosophy, "7 Amazing Ways to Love Yourself the Way You Are"[1]

"Two loves have made two different cities: self-love hath made a terrestrial city, which rises in contempt of God; and Divine Love hath made a celestial one, which rises in contempt of self. The former glories in itself — the latter in God."

— Saint Augustine, *City of God*

---

[1] Kate Gitman, "7 Amazing Ways to Love Yourself the Way You Are," *Womenosophy*, October 2019, https://womenosophy.com/ways-love-yourself-way-you-are.

"To thine own self be true!" Words of wisdom from a genius, right? Shakespeare said it, and he's right about everything! He also said, "It is not in the stars to hold our destiny, but in ourselves," right? If it's going to be, it's up to me, you know?

Oops, nope, Shakespeare was not a self-fulfillment guru. "To thine own self be true," is a turn of phrase spoken by Polonius, a treasonous, spineless toady who turns his back on his children, his prince, and his country to serve himself. He's being true to himself all right; unfortunately, he's a horrible human being. How about that other quote? Well, the real quote is, "The fault, dear Brutus, is not in our stars, but in ourselves, that we are underlings." Wanna guess who says this one? Cassius, who is trying to manipulate Brutus into murdering his best friend, Julius Caesar, so that Cassius can have better career success. Both the book/movie *The Fault in Our Stars* by John Green, and the play *Dear Brutus* by J.M. Barrie (of Peter Pan fame), get their titles from this line. But *The Fault in Our Stars* seems to repurpose the phrase to mean that, through no fault of our own, circumstances determine our fate, and the best we can do is just be decent people in them. *Dear Brutus*, on the other hand, makes a much more startling observation. Barrie's play focuses on a group of friends who all blame their dissatisfaction in life on their circumstances, but through an otherworldly experience, they all discover that the problem is really that they are all just bad people. Cassius' fault, dear Brutus, is not his circumstance, nor any lack of ambition … but that he is true to himself, and he is a murderer. Which poses some challenging questions. "You do you!" we're told. "You won't be happy unless you live your own truth!" people say. "Be yourself!" we hear. *But what if we're not good people?* If we're looking to find our own truth inside ourselves, we're not just looking to be good people, but good arbiters of truth and morality. We're looking to be our own gods. The problem is, as G. K. Chesterton puts it in *Orthodoxy*, "That Jones shall worship the god within him turns out ultimately to mean that Jones shall worship Jones." And what a bummer of a god Jones turns out to be.

I'm not going to say that you're a total jerkhole and need to stop being yourself — we'll end up in a different place than that for sure. But follow me a little while. We frequently run into the problem not that we trust too little in ourselves and miss out on happiness, but that we trust too much in the littlest, worst parts of ourselves, and get exactly what we deserve. I've noticed a growing tendency in our culture to think that we must not regret, must not admit mistakes. How often have you heard someone say (or said yourself), "Well sure, you know, XYZ might seem to you like a bad idea, or like I shouldn't have done it, but it made me who I am today, so I don't regret it. I wouldn't change anything about my life, so yeah, I'm glad it happened." I've heard people use this formula to say that they didn't regret their drug use, their abortion, their criminal past, their adultery … the list goes on. And it reveals a concerning way that we talk to ourselves about who we are and what we do: Instead of learning from our mistakes and regretting them as departures from our truest selves (or who we would like to be), we instead defend our mistakes and accept them as an authentic part of who we are. Heck, we don't just accept them; in our defensiveness, we wear them as a badge of honor! "Abortion's wrong, huh? Well, I've had an abortion/I got my girlfriend an abortion, and no one can tell me I was wrong to do it! I regret nothing! I'm glad I did it, otherwise I could never be who I am now!" Or: "No, I don't regret cheating on my girlfriend at the time. I mean, obviously it shows I was in the wrong relationship, and now I'm out of that one and I'm in the right one, and I'd never cheat on *her*!" I've met people who have used that line of reasoning to excuse their adultery in upwards of three past relationships. In at least one instance, I heard that statement, even including, "and I'd never cheat on her," followed shortly by the breakup of that relationship after he did, in fact, cheat on her, and determined that it too must not have been the right relationship. My theory on what was really happening? He refused to acknowledge that he has a problem faithfully keeping his word (or, shall I say, actually being true to himself), refused to repent of his mistakes, and therefore didn't learn from them. In fact, the only way for us to truly learn from our mistakes is to admit we were wrong and repent.

Again, I don't mention any of these to pass judgment on anyone, but rather to call us to do that difficult task of repenting. If you're struggling with the pain of any of these mistakes, or having difficulty even acknowledging them as mistakes, I encourage you to seek the freedom of repentance. No matter what you've done, there is forgiveness, there is healing, and there are resources to help you. For all of them, the Sacrament of Confession is a great place to start. Also, because of the prevalence of abortion, I'd like to specifically mention Rachel's Vineyard ministry. If you've been involved in an abortion — whether it was yours or someone else's and whether you're a woman or a man — they can help you find healing. That's what's at stake here. Christ says, "The Son of Man came to seek and to save the lost" (Lk 19:10). It is not our good deeds, our strength, our never-making-mistakes that *earn* us salvation. It's our sins and failings that prompt God to find us out, and to heal and save us by his love. If you can repent, you can find healing and peace. If you won't repent, you won't heal, plain and simple.

If that's true though, why then do we fight repentance and healing so hard? Tell me if this feels familiar to you: When it comes to my mistakes, I seem to be terrified that if I *do* admit I was wrong and repent, that I am somehow reduced as a person; that there's something wrong not just with my actions, but with who I am. But quite the opposite is true! The sooner we can admit and repent our mistakes, the more easily we show ourselves that those actions, that behavior, that wrongdoing, is not who we are. Our repentance, our contrition, and our pledge to do better are what define us, not our mistakes. Unless, of course, we cling to them and refuse to regret. There's an example of this from a ways back, at a famous little garden party. Maybe you've heard of it:

> The serpent said to the woman, "You will not die. For God knows that when you eat of [the fruit of the tree] your eyes will be opened, and you will be like God, knowing good and evil." So when the woman saw that the tree was good for food, and that it was a delight to the eyes, and that the tree was to be desired to make one wise, she took of its fruit and ate; and she also gave some to her husband, who was with her, and he ate. (Genesis 3:4–6)

Talk about a scam! The serpent told Adam and Eve that all they needed to do to be "like God" and "know good and evil" was to eat of the fruit of the tree. But hold on a second. They already know what's good — everything God has made, their union with him, and their union with each other. And hold on another second! If they eat the fruit, they can be "like God?" But they already are! "So God created man in his own image, in the image of God he created him; male and female he created them" (Gn. 1:27). God breathed his own Spirit into them (cf. Gn 2:7). They're the only beings in the universe who are like God! But instead of trusting God and knowing who he has made them to be, they trust the serpent, and who he says they are. They settled for the serpent's vision of them, and that changed them. It made them who they are today, if you will.

I have this impression (feel free to agree or disagree) that we are far more invested nowadays in settling for a really minimal vision of ourselves than we were, even in the recent past. In the

1980s and '90s there was an obsession with self-improvement across the board: physical improvement, mental improvement, career improvement, psychological healing, spiritual connection, etc. Now, I'm not saying we executed self-improvement well (it may have looked a lot more like *American Psycho* than *Pilgrim's Progress*), but the desire for self-improvement was there. Now we seem to prefer improvement of circumstances to improvement of self. After all, it takes much less effort to win the lottery than to work hard; to become Instagram famous than to earn a good reputation; to get liposuction or Botox or "freeze the fat" than to exercise and diet; to make a vision board and manifest than to humble ourselves before God. It's far easier for us to make ourselves content with where we are than to work every day to be better. We talk about "fat-shaming" during an obesity epidemic, and "slut-shaming" at a time when among 300 million Americans there are 110 million sexually transmitted infections.[2] We decry people being judgmental more than we decry the sins they judge. Why? Because if we shut down or cancel anyone holding people to a higher standard, we feel more justified in ignoring a higher standard for ourselves. Better to lower the bar than to improve our behavior. And so we tell everyone, "You're good enough just the way you are!" Actually, no, you're not. But that should be inspiring, not depressing. Because we can all be better. I'm not talking about "becoming a better version of yourself," or "being your best self," which seems generally just to reduce down to "Take time for you, so you can be chiller, more successful, more open to the universe, and stuff." I'm not even talking about the aforementioned *American Psycho* style of self-improvement. I'm not talking about your personality, or being goofy or nerdy or popular or whatever; I'm talking about holiness. I'm talking

---

[2] Nicholas Bakalar, "In the US, 110 Million STD Infections," *The New York Times,* September 29 2017, https://www.nytimes.com/2017/09/29/health/chlamydia-syphilis-gonorrhea.html.

about any time we are tempted to settle for who we think we are at this moment, any time we are tempted to identify our selves with our faults and our sins. What if in those moments, we instead identify with who we are called to be? Then we can see our faults and sins clearly for what they are: things that hold us back from being the people that God has made us. If I think in terms of being my "best self," I'm already on the wrong track. I begin to already let myself off the hook and presume that if I'm crappy to me and people around me, it's just not my best day or my best self, but it's still me. In other words, I'm giving room for my sins and shortcomings to define me.

There's no "best self" because there's only one self ... the authentic life God gave me. At the 1993 World Youth Day in Denver, Pope Saint John Paul II said, "Become who you are." This indicates (among other things) that we are not presently who we *really* are. And who is that? Well, to further quote JPII (in his Angelus address of December 15, 1996), we discover who we are in the mystery of Christ's Incarnation: "Christ is the light because, in his divine identity, he reveals the Father's face. But he is so too because, being a man like us and in solidarity with us in everything except sin, he reveals man to himself." Or as Saint Thomas Aquinas puts it, "The only-begotten Son of God, wanting to make us sharers in his divinity, assumed our nature, so that he, made man, might make men gods."

That's the great news. We are called not just to "be ourselves," which can so often mean settling for our sins. We are called to be who Christ has made us: Sharers in his divinity. We are called not to be content "just the way we are," but to find contentment in Christ, and be satisfied only by growing closer to him. We are called to grow more humble, more honest, more giving, more just, more merciful, more pure in heart, more peacemaking, more righteous every day from here to eternity, because eternity is our destiny. On that note, it might be worth mentioning the second half, the conclusion, of Chesterton's quote on Jones worshipping the God within. He says:

> Let Jones worship the sun or moon, anything rather than the Inner Light; let Jones worship cats or crocodiles, if he can find any in his street, but not the god within. Christianity came into the world firstly in order to assert with violence that a man had not only to look inwards, but to look outwards, to behold with astonishment and enthusiasm a divine company and a divine captain. The only fun of being a Christian was that a man was not left alone with the Inner Light, but definitely recognized an outer light, fair as the sun, clear as the moon, terrible as an army with banners.

And that's the conclusion I would leave you with: If we look within and see our brokenness (or perhaps even more necessarily if we *don't* see our brokenness), we shouldn't stop there and claim that as our own. For our own sanity, for our own well-being, for our own self-improvement, we must become who we are. The only way to do that is to look outward, to the God who made us and loves us, the God who reveals man to himself.

SO NOW WHAT?

- Are you feeling regret about anything? Well stop that right now! Justify it, rationalize it, move on!
- Or, if you'd like to allow some honesty and healing into your life, take some real time (minimum five minutes per session, maximum thirtyish per session) to engage in a hard look at your actions. Today, do an examen of your day. Tomorrow, think back further to the whole week. The next day, think back

a month or two. Then a year. Are there things that weigh on you? That affect you in some way and you don't quite know why? Are there things you find yourself habitually doing and you're just now realizing that you wish you weren't? Find a time to go to confession. If it might be a long confession, that's fine, just make a private appointment rather than trying to squeeze it in on a Saturday afternoon. Talk it out with the priest, and seek the further resources and support you need to give your shortcomings to Christ, and hold fast to him.

4
Get Some Tonight!

(How hookup culture cripples our ability to love)

"Use these passion-packed phrases to get her into bed tonight. ... The right words and gestures, after all, can seal the deal, while the wrong ones can break it. So don't leave anything to chance."

— Men's Health, "6 Phrases to Get Her Into Bed Tonight"[1]

"Don't you long to shout to those youths who are bustling around you: Fools! Leave those worldly things that shackle the heart – and very often degrade it – leave all that and come with us in search of Love!"

— Saint Josemaría Escrivá, *The Way*

---

[1] Nicole Beland, "6 Phrases to Get Her into Bed Tonight," *Men's Health*, 2 April 2015, https://www.menshealth.com/sex-women/a19536318/get-her-into-bed/.

Stop me if you've heard this one ...

- "Sex is natural!"
- "Love is love!"
- "Everyone wants it, it would be wrong not to have sex!"
- "You can't really know if you're compatible with someone until you know you're sexually compatible!"
- "Love and sex just go together, you know?"

Or maybe you've heard some of these:
- "Look, sex and love are two different things."
- "I'm really just looking to score right now."
- "We both want it, so who cares if it's just for one night?"
- "Netflix and chill?"

Or perhaps one of these sounds familiar:

- "Then I found out he was a total man-whore."
- "OMG, what a slut."
- "Slut-shaming has to stop."
- "Don't player-hate, congratulate!" (OK, probably no one has said that one specifically since maybe 1999, but the sentiment is still there.)

And maybe, just maybe, you've heard or seen one of these:

- #metoo
- #timesup
- #yesallwomen

Why am I running through a litany of cultural tropes on sex? Well, it seems to me that if one tries to discern our culture's attitude toward sex, it isn't wrong so much as it's completely unintelligible. Or maybe it's both wrong and unintelligible. If we try to lay out some "rules" on sex from our culture, the list would probably look like this:

1. Everyone wants sex. Sex is always good to do and you shouldn't feel any shame about it, no matter whom (or how many whoms) it is with, so long as they are both/all consenting adults. Or, if they're not adults, that's fine, as long as you're not either. Oh, and be safe. Condoms and pills for everyone.

2. "Good guys" don't pressure women into sex — but that's why good guys never get any. "Good girls" don't put out — but that's why they never have any fun. No matter what you do in the bedroom (or what number of bedrooms you do it in), you're a good person, so long as you follow rule #1.

3. You might not like sex with a particular partner, or they might be bad at it, so try it with as many people as you like until you find someone you really click with. You wouldn't buy a car without test-driving it and probably a couple others, would you? And while you might not like sex with a particular partner, never, under any circumstances, regret having sex with someone. See "sex is always good to do," above. Unless you were drunk or your consent was impaired in some other way, but that's a whole other issue. In fact, while we're on the topic of regret, never regret anything you ever do, because it's made you who you are today.

4. Remember, sex is about fun, not just love; so do it if

it's fun and don't if it's not. Until it's about love, and then it's about both. Oh, just so there's no confusion: In the vernacular, "love" = sex. Love is love, no matter how you express it. But love doesn't have to be a part of "love" if you don't want it to, or it can if you do want it to, or if you need it to sound that way for the purposes of your agenda. Because who doesn't like love? Love is great, right? We can all agree on that. Back to the point, if sex is ever not fun, don't do it. And don't worry about getting accustomed to having sex with different or multiple partners. If you want to settle down later on, you shouldn't have any problem with doing that. This whole period of sowing your wild oats will have absolutely no effect on you so long as you do the whole safe-sex thing. And get tested. Cuz, let's be honest, even the safe-sex thing still only works so-so. But don't worry, there will be absolutely, positively, zero emotional fallout from having sex any time, anywhere, with anybody (or any number of anybodies) so long as it was consensual.

5. OK, yeah, that's everything. Pretty much. For now. Maybe. This could change at any moment, TBH. Got it? Good. Just get out there and have fun, and NEVER BREAK THE RULES.

So ... how are these rules working out for us? Well, here's few data points:

- In the United States (depending on how you tabulate it) somewhere between 35–50 percent of marriages end in divorce.[2]

- Each year, about 1 in 4 pregnancies end in abortion.[3]
- One in three women and one in six men is a victim of sexual violence at some point in their lives.[4]
- One in five women is a victim of rape. Of those women, 51 percent were raped by an intimate partner, 40.8 percent by an acquaintance.[5]

I'd like to share some anecdotal points as well, some of which might ring true to you. And again, if anything rings so true it makes you uncomfortable, please know that I'm bringing it up not to mock or judge, but hopefully so that you and I can see our lives honestly, and honestly open ourselves to grace. In the *Summa Theologiae*, Saint Thomas Aquinas says that when we're talking sin with a sinner, "If we find that we are guilty of the same sin, we must not rebuke him, but groan with him, and invite him to repent with us." Trust me, in this book I'm never rebuking you, I'm groaning with you, and hoping we can repent together. OK, all that said, here we go.

I've talked to men and women alike who, while they may talk about past sexual encounters as though they're just things of the

[2] CDC/NCHS, "National Marriage and Divorce Rates 2018," https://www.cdc.gov/nchs/data/dvs /national-marriage-divorce-rates-00-18.pdf. See also, PolitiFact New Jersey, "Steve Sweeney claims two-thirds of marriages end in divorce," *Truth-O-Meter*, https://www.politifact.com/ factchecks/2012/feb/20/stephen-sweeney/steve-sweeney-claims-more-two-thirds-marriages-end/.
[3] Special tabulations of updated data from Sedgh G et al., Abortion incidence between 1990 and 2014: global, regional, and subregional levels and trends, *Lancet*, 2016, 388(10041):258–267. Accessed on Guttmacher Institute website, https://www.guttmacher.org/fact-sheet/induced-abortion -worldwide.
[4] Smith, S. G., Chen, J., Basile, K. C., Gilbert, L. K., Merrick, M. T., Patel, N., ... Jain, A. The National Intimate Partner and Sexual Violence Survey (NISVS): 2010-2012 state report. Retrieved from the Centers for Disease Control and Prevention, National Center for Injury Prevention and Control, https://www.cdc.gov/violenceprevention/pdf/NISVS-StateReportBook.pdf.
[5] Basile, K. C., Zhang, X., Smith, S.G., Wang, J., Merrick, M. T., Kresnow, M., Chen, J. The National Intimate Partner and Sexual Violence Survey (NISVS): 2015 Data Brief - Updated Release. Retrieved from the Centers for Disease Control and Prevention, National Center for Injury Prevention and Control, https://www.cdc.gov/violenceprevention/pdf/2015data-brief508.pdf.

past with no emotional attachment, *are still talking about them.* And if they talk for any length of time about these past encounters, I've nearly always heard a certain amount of regret begin to bubble up. Almost no one says, "I'm glad I tested out sexual relationships with a bunch of human beings whom I didn't realize I was just test-driving at the time. I really thought it could work — and then our relationship fell apart. But no big deal, right? The sexual aspect definitely made it easier to break up and easier to move on." The way you do hear people talk about it, however, is as if it's an unavoidable part of life. "Yeah, look it's too bad I still sometimes think of sex with my ex-girlfriend when I'm having sex with my current girlfriend, but what are you supposed to do? There's literally no solution! Except not having sex, I guess. BAHAHA! Scientifically impossible." I had a friendquaintance explain to me, "I love my wife. She's the only woman I've ever really loved. She's the mother of my kids. I hit the jackpot with her! But yeah, the girlfriend I had before her? The sex was better. Best I've ever had. And it's fine, my wife knows that, and she knows I love her." What? Your wife knows you prefer sex with a different woman, and she's fine with that? I don't buy that.

Even if a past encounter "meant nothing," or was part of a bad relationship, it still has an effect. In our society, we totally buy that the things we do, the self-talk we have, and the way we treat ourselves all affect our psyche … except sex. We believe that making our bed in the morning can make us a success in our lives; that standing in a "power position" can ace interviews and win negotiations; that what we conceive in our minds we can achieve in reality. But we somehow dismiss *all of that* when it comes to sex. In other words, we refuse to acknowledge that what we do in bed affects the rest of our lives; that putting ourselves in a position with one person affects how we deal with other people, and that what we conceive *is* reality that takes on a life of its own.

Some people (mostly men) balked at #yesallwomen, in which

women shared stories of sexual harassment, unwanted sexual advances or contact, violence, and intimidation; the implication being that *all women* have experienced at least one of the things on this list. I think the people who balked did so for one of three reasons. They either thought that it wasn't true that all women had experienced unwanted sexual attention; thought that the implication was that all men gave unwanted sexual attention (which is not, in fact, logically implied); or that it implied that men didn't also receive unwanted sexual attention (which it also doesn't imply). When I first heard of #yesallwomen, the simple assertion shocked me to some extent too. Wait, *all women*? But then I started thinking about things I had heard women say in conversation, things they mentioned in passing about their day, or the way they had to think about certain situations. Almost every adult woman I knew well had been catcalled at some point, and none of them liked it. Many women had experienced at least low-level stalking, knowing that a guy was figuring out where he could find them at work or out and about, sometimes finding their home and just showing up. Many of them had felt the need to take what seemed to me like unreasonable precautions coming and going from work to be safe, like walking mace in hand after a coworker had been assaulted, or even just wearing a hat and long coat in the summer because attractive women got followed in the area. A shockingly high number of women I knew had experienced what I judged to be terrifying encounters that guys somehow thought were appropriate. One woman I knew was run off the road while driving, only to have the guy pull over, shout through his open window that she was hot, and then drive off. Another received FaceTime requests, hangup calls, and explicit or threatening texts all from the same number. Is it *all* women? There's no possible way for anyone to know, but it certainly seems like it's happened in some form to all the women I know.

Perhaps you remember how, in the middle of all the #metoo lawsuits and allegations, Aziz Ansari was accused of sexual misconduct by a woman (referred to as "Grace"), who felt pressured into sex by him, touched in ways she didn't want, and said that she had spent the entire evening trying to send signals that this was way too much too fast. Ansari, particularly given his frequent comedy stylings specifically on relationships and treating women better, ran into a lot of blowback. But some people criticized Grace for remaining in a protracted situation where she was uncomfortable. Others then criticized those people for victim-blaming.

Perhaps you also remember Henry Cavill commenting on the #metoo movement to GQ Australia interviewer Adam Baidawi. Comments like this:

- "There's something wonderful about a man chasing a woman. There's a traditional approach to that, which is nice. I think a woman should be wooed and chased, but maybe I'm old-fashioned for thinking that."
- "It's very difficult to do that if there are certain rules in place. Because then it's like: 'Well, I don't want to go up and talk to her, because I'm going to be called a rapist or something.' … I'm someone in the public eye, and if I go and flirt with someone, then who knows what's going to happen?"
- "Now? Now you really can't pursue someone further than, 'No'. It's like, 'OK, cool'. But then there's the, 'Oh why'd you give up?' And it's like, 'Well, because I didn't want to go to jail?'"[6]

---

[6] Adam Baidawi, "Henry Cavill on His Best Life Lessons," *GQ Australia*, 10 July, 2018, https://www.gq.com.au/entertainment/celebrity/henry-cavill/image-gallery/faed7f272f09bdf899c92b63a7149cba.

One more anecdotal thing that might seem out of left field, but here it goes: FOMO is a thing. We spend a massive amount of time not committing to or flaking on events and people because we think something better might come along, and we're terrified of missing out. This is prevalent enough across our culture that we have developed the term Fear of Missing Out, and given it its own acronym. We have a serious problem with commitment, both making and keeping.

Now that I've presented all those data points and anecdotal points, let's dive deeper. I think every single one of these things is related (plus about a dozen more points we don't have time for), all because we refuse to acknowledge what sex is. We'd much rather treat it like it's whatever we want to be. But that's just wrong. If it were really true, for instance, that sex doesn't have to mean anything; or that it only has the meaning we ascribe to it; or it can just be something people do for fun and nothing more — then infidelity wouldn't be an issue; sexual assault and rape simply wouldn't even exist as concepts; and you wouldn't be able to have life-altering, shame-filled violations or major regrets. Phrased differently: We only have these intense emotional experiences surrounding sex because not only does sex have meaning in and of itself, but also because there are inherent right and wrong ways of doing it. When we use something contrary to its purpose, we experience negative consequences — and this applies to just about everything in the world. If I try to use my hand as a hammer, I'll hurt myself. Conversely, if we see negative consequences arising from an action, we can infer that there is, in fact, a way to use it correctly and a way to use it wrongly, and that we're currently using it wrongly. The pain I feel in my hand after smacking it on the head of a nail indicates that my hand is not meant to be used as a hammer. So, if nothing else, the fact that we see dozens of ways in which just about everyone has experienced sex as a wounding thing rather than a life-giving thing indicates that there is a pervasive wrongness in how we're doing it.

How do we know sex ought to be a life-giving action? Well, let's look at it from just a biological/evolutionary standpoint for one second (again, we seem to love taking that perspective for diet, fitness, motivation, productivity — pretty much everything except sex). Why do we have sexual desires and experience sexual pleasure? Biologically and evolutionarily it's to fulfill the purpose of our reproductive system and continue our species. We have a circulatory system, nervous system, cardiovascular system, digestive system, and muscular system that all fully function on their own. But the only way for the reproductive system to fulfill its purpose is in union with the reproductive system of someone of the opposite sex. From a scientific perspective then, sex exists for baby-making. In that context, the only way that sex fulfills its purpose is when it is between a man and a woman, and most functionally in a period of fertility. We'll talk in a minute about the differences between working in concert with our bodies' systems, treating them optimally, treating them sub-optimally, and working contrary to them. What we have said so far is simply to give us a clear idea of the purely natural end of sex and our sexual desires.

Even if we continue to stick to the natural and keep God, the sanctity of the human person, and the immortal soul out of the discussion completely, we can start at least from the scientific perspective to see where we are going wrong. Where the rest of our bodily systems are concerned, we recognize the physiological and psychological issues caused not just by using them contrary to their biological purpose, but also by not treating them optimally. For example, bulimia is one way of directly using the digestive system contrary to its purpose. Anorexia, overeating, and maintaining a poor diet are other ways of using our digestive system sub-optimally that are still destructive both physiologically and psychologically. In the nervous system, chronic substance abuse can do irreparable damage, while even "minor" drunkenness or highness can lead us to destructive actions. So, even though you aren't forced to follow the biological framework for any of your body's systems, you can acknowledge that there are ways your body and mind thrive, and a multitude of ways they don't. If that's true for all the rest of your body's systems, how could it be false for your reproductive system?

In order to posit that, we have to appeal to something outside of the logical or scientific perspective. Now, for humans at least, there is something beyond just the logical and scientific perspective that factors into treating sex rightly or wrongly. It's not something that reduces our responsibilities around sex, rather it increases them. How do we know this? Take a look at other animals. In other animals, "infidelity" isn't a thing, because "fidelity" isn't a thing. While a very small amount of animal species may "mate for life," this generally only means that a male/female pair shares the duties of raising young, and doesn't actually correlate to sexual monogamy.[7] Plus, animals aren't concerned with consent, and don't seem to experience lasting psychological trauma from non-consensual encounters. The fact that animals' experience of sex is so different from ours seems to indicate that for humans, there's something beyond just biology going on.

I'm going to reference the "4 F's" now, otherwise known as the four pillars. They can all be found conceptually in the *Catechism of the Catholic Church* (cf. 2331–2400). Beyond the simple biology of it, we can know through reason and experience that sex is designed to be a *free, full, faithful, fruitful* gift of self. In fact, sex is only actually sex when it is all of these things. For us to properly understand sex, we have to stop referring to all genital activity as "sex." If it's not freely chosen, it's coercion, assault, or

---

[7] Jeffrey Black, *Partnerships in Birds: The Study of Monogamy* (Oxford: Oxford University Press, 1996), 323.

rape. If it's not full, it's fornication. If it's not faithful, it's adultery. If it's not fruitful, it may be masturbation or even activity that leads to abortion. Let's unpack these one at a time.

Free

We have the instinct that sex is meant to be a gift, since we know how strongly we want to freely give it, as opposed to have it *taken* from us. Humans experience deep pain and abiding trauma from unwanted or coerced sexual activity. I would posit that the exact reason we are crushed right now by a pervasive culture of sexual assault, harassment, unwanted attention, and even the fear surrounding it that (for instance) Henry Cavill said he felt, is because we treat sex as something to *get*, not a gift to give and a gift to freely receive. We talk about "getting some," "getting laid," "smashing that" … all self-centered, self-driven actions that come from a place of taking, rather than mutually free giving and receiving. If a man is trying to get something from a woman, it is only natural that she would experience the pain of use that that implies. As an analogously related example: My friend, Patrick Dwyer, is a really skilled singer-songwriter (seriously, check him out on Spotify), but also a really skilled film editor. He has friends who will only call him when they want him to edit something for free. "Hey man, it's been a long time! We should catch up soon! While I've got you here though, I have this short film and we've been looking for an editor, but you know, we don't have a budget at all. We're all just doing this to try to further our careers. There's no money in it right this second and … " Unless they want something out of him, he doesn't hear from them. Many of us may have had similar experiences of being used, and it doesn't feel good. In fact, in *Love and Responsibility*, Cardinal Karol Wojtyla (the future Pope Saint John Paul II) intimates that use, rather than hate, is the opposite of love, "A person's rightful due is to be treated as an object of love, not as an object for use."

This use, this attempt to *get some* from someone, dehumanizes the other person. Instead of receiving a gift of love, they find themselves reduced to the role of a tool for someone else to *get off.*

Full

We know in our hearts and in our experience that sex is always a communication of self. If we pay attention to the language of that communication — the language of our bodies — we see that it ought to be not only a free gift of self, but a *full* gift of self. Again, from a biological perspective, the completion of the reproductive system only happens through a full unity of man and woman; and so even on a base level, I think we have this sense that sex ought to be the culmination of relationship, an honest expression of fullness, not the starting point of relationship or entirely divorced from relationship. We see the fallout from ignoring this instinct, this voice of our hearts, in many ways. Look, for instance, at the high rates of breakup in cohabiting couples. They have a separation rate up to five times higher than that of married couples, and reconcile only one-third as frequently as their married counterparts.[8] This is one of the problems of pretending one has made a full gift of self without actually having done it. In addition, cohabiting couples also tend to stay in bad relationships longer (that eventually end anyway) than they believe they would have otherwise. As clinical psychologist Meg Jay puts it, "I have clients who say 'I spent years of my 20s living with someone who I wouldn't have dated a year if we had not been living together.' … Once you buy dishes, share a lease, have a routine, and get a dog, it can be difficult to cut your losses and accept that the rela-

---

[8] Sheri Stritoff, "Essential Cohabitation Facts and Statistics," *The Spruce*, 14 August, 2019, https://www.thespruce.com/cohabitation-facts-and-statistics-2302236.

tionship isn't working."[9]

The high rates of divorce we have in the United States are a further indication that the way we are doing marriage isn't a *full* gift of self either. If we really mean and hold fast to wedding vows, we promise a full gift of our entire lives, not just chronologically, but substantially! You're not just promising to hang around until one of you drops dead, you're promising to give the other person everything you've got. To love and honor, to be true in good times and in bad, in sickness and in health, all the days of your life, every single one. That's a full gift of self, and doesn't leave room for parting ways somewhere in the middle (and remember, I'm saying this as someone who has gone through a divorce and annulment ... more on this on the chapter on marriage, by the way). I'll add emphasis to this quote of Jesus, "Have you not read that he who made them from the beginning made them male and female, and said, 'For this reason a man shall leave his father and mother and be joined to his wife, and the two shall become one flesh'? *So they are no longer two, but one.* What therefore God has joined together, let no man put asunder" (Mt 19:4–6, emphasis added). Everything about the act of sex indicates fullness of unity, and as the departures from fullness indicate, we experience both short- and long-term consequences any time we try to ignore that. Our bodies and our hearts won't be fooled by false narratives, and they won't settle for casual treatment. This leads us right to fidelity.

Faithful

"Man is the only creature on earth which God willed for itself, [and he] cannot fully find himself except through a sincere gift

[9] Lauren Fox, "The Science of Cohabitation," *The Atlantic*, 20 March, 2014, https://www.theatlantic.com/health/archive/2014/03/the-science-of-cohabitation-a-step-toward-marriage-not-a-rebellion/284512/

of himself."[10] In understanding our desire to both be a full gift of self and receive another as a full gift of their self, we are led to the topic of fidelity. Because if we become one flesh with another in the sexual act, in a full union of selves, how can we share that fullness of unity with more people? That physical union precludes any rivals. There are plenty of scientific arguments that humans are wired to want fidelity: the release of the "bonding hormones" oxytocin and vasopressin, the human chemistry changes that support childbearing with one specific partner, etc. However, we also have negative evidence that proves this desire and need for faithfulness. We find this evidence both in our emotional experience of not having fidelity, and through the indelibly lingering connection to past partners.

Have you ever been cheated on? Whether or not sex was involved, has someone you believed to be committed to you given attention to someone else in a way that seemed to violate that exclusive commitment? I have experienced infidelity in the past, and it feels downright awful. Sometimes, to try to protect ourselves, we'll attempt to find ways to excuse it if it happens to us, or downplay it, but we can't undo the brokenness or the destruction of trust we experience. Frequently, that distrust then extends to all other persons of the same gender as the one who broke our trust — for example, women who say, "all men are liars," or guys who go, "ugh, I'm swearing off women!" Even people who have been unfaithful still experience pain when the situation is reversed. In fact, I think every person I have known who admits to (or, distressingly, sometimes brags about) having broken fidelity in a relationship has also at some point in their lives been the victim of infidelity, and admits how awful it feels. Even when they are willing to excuse it, discount it, or do it themselves, they still

---

[10] Vatican Council II, *Gaudium Et Spes*, www.vatican.va/archive/hist_councils/ii_vatican_council /documents/vat-ii_cons_19651207_gaudium-et-spes_en.html, par. 24.

hate it when it happens to them.

Further, if there is intra-relationship fidelity, an odd, un-comfortable connection seems to remain, tying one to past sexual partners long after they are gone. It's as if this desire for fidelity is something that applies not just to one relationship, but to life. We all seem to prefer that there are no previous attachments hanging on to the person with whom we decide to make a lifelong commitment. As Gwen Stefani sings in No Doubt's *In My Head*, "Don't talk about ex-girlfriends, don't talk about you without me, don't talk about your past." Now, she's obviously not asking him to eschew conversation about his childhood, or the fun he had at Disney World in eighth grade, or the sandwich he bought the day before he met her. She's asking to know that he is giving her his whole heart and his whole self, and not holding anything back for someone else. And that's the hard truth here: There's no "casual" way to give yourself to someone else. That's why those bonds nag at us even when we think we've moved on, and why in our hearts, we really long to give ourselves not merely to one person, but to one person once and for all.

Fruitful

In many ways, this should be the most easily discernible one. Yet we have done an incredible job as a culture of brainwashing ourselves into ignoring the blatantly obvious connection between *sex* and *babies*. It's the *only* biological or evolutionary reason for the sexual drive, sexual pleasure, and a sexual reproductive system; and the fact that a materialist society would try to deny that borders on insanity. If reproduction is the natural end of sex, then if we try to separate sex from reproduction we are directly working *against* our biology, our evolutionary function, and our instincts. People often talk about keeping God out of the bedroom, when in fact we must (odd as it might sound) invite God our Creator into the bedroom if we expect sex to be more than simply reproduction. The materialist argument for reducing sex to the purely natural essentially says, "Well, I try not to bring religion into eating, so I think if you want to eat only Twinkies and then throw them up, that makes total sense. You only need to take in calories if you *want* to. You do you." No, we know that if we separate our drives from their natural ends the consequences aren't good — except, we try to convince ourselves, when it comes to sex. And so, while there are other divinely revealed ends to sex (the strengthening and living out of the marriage bond, participation in God's creative action, etc.), none of those take away the *natural* end of making babies. As the *Catechism* says: "Conjugal love naturally tends to be fruitful. A child does not come from outside as something added on to the mutual love of the spouses, but springs from the very heart of that mutual giving, as its fruit and fulfillment" (2366). This natural end of fruitfulness is one of the reasons why the Church still teaches against contraception, masturbation, and homosexual acts despite society's cries of outdated, backwards thinking. In reality, it's backwards to try to separate our biological processes and necessities from their natural ends; it's not backwards to uphold them. All of these things that attempt to work against the natural end of our sexual design or fruitfulness also end up working against fullness too, and by degrees turn us away from a gift of self, and back onto a focus on self.[11]

• • •

The further we move away from a free, full, faithful, and fruitful gift of self, the further we move from the fulfillment of our deep-

---

[11] If you are specifically interested in the concept of responsible parenthood without contraception, I encourage you to listen to Dr. Janet Smith's talk "Contraception - Why Not?," to read *Humanae Vitae* by Pope Saint Paul VI, and to learn about how Natural Family Planning (NFP), when exercised responsibly and for the right reasons, can deepen communication and openness in marriage.

est desires of giving and receiving love. We don't actually have to look hard to see why ... or rather, we wouldn't have to if our society hadn't spent so much time and effort trying to convince us that our actions needn't have consequences. As humans, we do a great job of distancing ourselves from the natural consequences of our actions, and believing that the artificial distance reduces our culpability. One time when I heard Christopher West speak on the Theology of the Body, he briefly related the story of David. As a quick refresher, David, a shepherd boy, is anointed to become the second king of Israel after Saul. He's the only Israelite who trusts God's protection enough to fight Goliath, and he saves Israel from the Philistines. David becomes super popular, which scares King Saul, who thinks he'll be overthrown early and decides to kill David. David escapes and becomes a great warrior. Saul dies, David becomes King. Then, one fateful day, David is walking on the roof of his palace, as one does, and sees a lady named Bathsheba taking a bath. He likes what he sees, so he has her husband Uriah sent to the front lines of battle and killed, and adds Bathsheba to his stock of wives. But he takes no responsibility for her husband's death ... even though his whole purpose in sending him into battle was to get him killed! He takes so little responsibility in fact, that when the prophet Nathan tells King David a parable of a man with many sheep who murdered another man to take the one and only sheep that man owned and loved, David doesn't even get that the story is about him! Nathan has to go, "Uh ... David, you're the murderer in the story. Duh." As all of us in Christopher West's audience nodded to ourselves about what an idiot David was, and how glad we were that in modern times men take responsibility for their actions, West followed up with, "But after all, how many men today are willing to commit murder to indulge their lusts?" *Well, you know, rapist/ murderers, I guess*, was my thought, and based on the slightly confused looks of people around me, I assumed their thoughts were running a similar track. "Millions," he said in answer to his own question. People in the audience started looking at each other, presumably wondering which among us fell into this "millions of murderers" category. "How many men, to indulge their lust for a woman, will murder their own *child*? How many men procure an abortion so they can indulge their lust instead of accepting the responsibility of love?" *Oh that's what he meant. Oh dear. Millions is right.*

King David isn't the only man (or only person) who would rather take than give, who treated other people as objects to satisfy his desires, who tried to casually attach himself to dozens of lovers. This is the disease plaguing our culture. We believe we can "hook up," and then just move on. Yet every single time we do, we further cripple our ability to truly love. We move on away from love, towards selfishness, distrust, pain, anger, fear, degrading others and ourselves, objectifying them to satisfy our desires. Unfortunately, none of these counterfeits can satisfy our desires, so the hunger grows worse until some are willing to kill for it.

Does any of this sound familiar? Maybe you've experienced frustration and fear in your relationships, a lack of commitment from your partner or the inability to commit yourself. Maybe after a date you find yourself experiencing this nagging regret, or just feeling dirty. Maybe King David's story feels all too close to home, and the prophet Nathan seems to be speaking to you when he says sadly, "You are that man." What, then, are you to do? Shrug it off? Say, "Well, I guess that's who I am now?" Despair? No! None of the above. Here we can take a different lesson from David: not a negative one but a positive one. When David hears Nathan's words, when he realizes that he has taken the gifts of God and abused them, shown ingratitude in the face of blessing, and indulged in the selfishness of lust instead of the selflessness of love, what does he do? First, he confesses. "David said to Nathan, 'I have sinned against the Lord'" (2 Sm 12:13). He repents, he asks for God's mercy, and vows to go and sin no more. And no matter our own sins, no matter their magnitude, we too can ask for and receive the mercy of God, if only we repent.

Now that doesn't mean it will be easy. While God grants David mercy and forgives his sin, he doesn't take away the consequences of David's actions. David still has much hard reckoning to do to "go and sin no more." Bathsheba miscarries and David loses his son, David's other wives reject him, relationships fall apart, and his selfishness and refusal to love alienates his children and brings conflict deeply into his family, and he struggles much of his days to reconcile with them. But David saves and grows his closest relationships, and he learns to love even those who don't love him, to love and not count the cost — in short, to love like God. And he never could have learned that love or experienced that freedom if he had held on to his sin and let it define him.

We have the same challenge before us: Learning to love will not come without cost. This might take very hard conversations with your girlfriend or boyfriend, or perhaps your spouse, if you find a part of your relationship that isn't full, free, faithful, and fruitful. This may take a support group, or accountability partners if you find that you struggle with habitual issues like pornography or masturbation. It may mean that a relationship will end. Repentance isn't easy, but it's necessary, and it'll be worth it. I spent nearly a decade of my life trying to justify pornography and masturbation. I found no freedom there. I spent several years trying to justify a relationship where both of us acted out of selfishness almost all the time. After many hard conversations, that relationship ended in a divorce and annulment. I've found that freedom and love were, have been, and are only able to exist in my life inasmuch as I'm willing to repent, to give of myself, and not count the cost. None of those are easy, and they all take work every single day; but they're absolutely worth it! I'm certainly not saying I'm perfect — I wouldn't have to repent daily if I were! I'm saying that the work of love brings me much more joy and freedom than indulging in anything less than love. And that brings us back to the question of those counterfeits for love — lust, selfishness, "hook up" culture, porn, etc. The counterfeits can't satisfy our longings. If only we can lean into love though, real love, our desires can be met. If we treat love and the physical expression of it as an opportunity to give ourselves fully, freely, faithfully, and fruitfully, these counterfeits appear clearly for the frauds they are, and only the good now appeals. Thus, in holding out for that which does satisfy, we come to fully find ourselves in the sincere gift of ourselves. And that is a gift indeed.

SO NOW WHAT?

- Love is love, right? Just define it how you want and do what you want - go get 'em tiger! Except never break the unspoken rules from the beginning of this chapter!
- Or, if there's something in the words of Saint Josemaría Escrivá, "Leave those worldly things that shackle the heart — and very often degrade it — leave all that and come with us in search of Love!" that speaks to you, do something about it.

  1. First, examine your conscience. Find those places where you've fallen for the less-than, where your love hasn't been full, free, faithful, or fruitful.
  2. Next, repent and confess it ... bring what was done in the darkness out into the light.

3. Finally, ask yourself, "What do I need to do to really go and sin no more?" Does it mean a hard conversation (or multiple hard conversations) with your significant other? Are you and your boyfriend or girlfriend actually an impediment to each other's growth and need to go your separate ways, even if (or especially if) that means you'd move out, give up a comfortable relationship, and feel like you're "losing out?" Does sinning no more mean staying off Instagram or the internet in general for a while? Do you need a close friend or family member to be honest with and accountable to in regards to your habits? Does it mean taking more time to fill your mind and heart with the good instead of the "meh, good enough" — for example, reading the Bible daily, going to adoration or Mass, receiving the Eucharist and the sacraments more often, etc.? Start with one challenging way of living love, and keep moving forward. Remember, repentance and love are things we must do *daily* if we expect to do them at all.

5

Opposite-Sex Besties Are the Best!

(How we're emotionally using the people we care about)

"A reminder that men and women can be friends. *Just* friends."

— *Huffington Post Wellness,* "10 Things Everyone with an Opposite-Sex Bestie Knows to Be True"[1]

"Love everyone with a strenuous love based on charity, but form friendships only with those who can share virtuous things with you."

— St. Francis De Sales, *Introduction to the Devout Life*

---

[1] Kelsey Borrenson, "10 Things Everyone with an Opposite-Sex Bestie Knows to Be True," *Huffington Post,* November 15, 2016, https://www.huffpost.com/entry/opposite-sex-best-friends_n_582b49ade4b0e39c1fa6717f.

The Huffington Post quote above is from an article called "10 Things Everyone with an Opposite-Sex Bestie Knows to Be True." Numbers 2 and 9 will blow your mind! Just kidding. But I do think a couple of points in that article deserve a closer look. The first statement that really caught my attention is, "The friendship isn't a threat to our romantic relationships"; and the second one is, "It's possible to be affectionate with your bestie in a completely platonic way." The person being quoted on that one explains that while they will sometimes sleep in the same bed, cuddle, show affection, etc., since there's no sexual attraction there, there's no problem. We're going to get much more into this in a second, but whether we're talking physical intimacy or emotional intimacy, if you're sharing that with someone other than the person you're in a romantic relationship with, yes, there definitely is a problem. Let me explain.

In high school and college, I had several close female friends. I would probably even say best friends, at various times. At one point or another, one of us "caught feelings," as they say. Every time. The relationship started with a mutual friendzoning, but it just didn't stay there. Now, fortunately or unfortunately — depending on how you look at it — it always happened that it was only one or the other of us who started feeling more for the other person, so none of them became romantic relationships ... but they all ceased being close friendships. After a certain point of noticing this progression of friendship → close friendship → best friends! → oops, someone got interested → let's just go back to the way it was and save this friendship → darn, nope, that's not gonna work → OK, see you around I guess, I realized that maybe, just maybe, there was a pattern here. One of us (sometimes it was me, sometimes it was the "her" involved) always ended up not being able to be "just friends." So, after a half-dozen or so "best friendships" crashed and burned, I decided to stop cultivating close friendships with women. It just wasn't doing either of us any favors. It might be worth mentioning here how I'm defining "close friendships/best friendships." In my vocabulary, these would be *any* (not necessarily all) of the following:

- Friendships where you intentionally spend one-on-one time with each other: It's just the two of you.
- Relationships where you talk to the person about your romantic interests.
- Friendships where you "can talk about anything," including personal things that you wouldn't talk about if there were others around. Even if you go, "Yeah, I've got three friends like this, so if it were the four of us all hanging out together, I'd still talk about personal things," this still counts, because it demonstrates that you have a high level of emotional intimacy with this person.
- Relationships where you give gestures of affection that you wouldn't give if they were of the same sex.

Any of this ringing true for you? Have you had any of these kinds of relationships and found yourself catching feelings? Or found the other person looking at you that way? Maybe not ... maybe I'm the only person who's hit speed bumps in having opposite-sex besties. Only I don't think that I am.

I can't count the number of times I've talked to both men and women who've (sometimes in the space of one conversation) said that their closest friends are of the opposite sex, and then also bemoaned the fact that they're having a hard time finding or maintaining a romantic relationship. I can't count the number of times, but I can tell you that it's 100 percent. One hundred percent of people I've known who've had an opposite-sex bestie experience difficulties in their romantic relationship, or experience difficulties even getting into a romantic relationship. Zero percent blame themselves or their best friends. They all blame their romantic partners, their potential theoretical romantic partners, fate, or God.

So in those instances I always mention my own experience, and that I realized my "best friends" of the past and I weren't doing ourselves any favors by having this close emotional bond that was "just friends." I get several responses in return:

- "What? That can't be the problem. We're just friends! My girlfriend/boyfriend is just jealous, that's the problem."
- "What? How could my friendship be the problem? Me being friends with a girl is no different than me being friends with a guy!"
- "What? No way is that a problem! She's like my sister/he's like my brother!"
- "What? That's not the problem. We're just friends, we're not doing anything."

This last one is sometimes immediately followed by, "I mean sure, we've made out/had sex a few times, but that was a long time ago, it's not like that now!" or "I mean sure, we'll cuddle sometimes or kiss sometimes or sleep in the same bed or whatever, but it's just like, in a friendly way." *Cue my raised eyebrow.* "Ugh, I knew you wouldn't understand! It's, you know, just totally *platonic* spooning and back massages and head massages and foot massages and mostly-cheek-sometimes-lips-kissing … platonic!"

In all of these I'm reminded of a scene from the original *Jumanji* (by far the superior film. Sorry, Mr. Rock, sir), where the young boy Peter receives this verse from the game, "A law of Jumanji has been broken. You will slip back even more than your token."

With this, his companions realize he tried to out-scheme the game, and grown-up Sarah asks, "You tried to cheat?"

"No," Peter replies, "I tried to drop the dice so they'd land on twelve."

"Oh, OK honey, well that would be cheating."

Peter fooled himself, and he might have been able to fool Sarah, but he couldn't fool Jumanji. In the same way, sometimes we can fool ourselves, sometimes we can fool friends, boyfriends, or girlfriends. But no matter who gets fooled, it doesn't change the nature of male-female relationships, and relationships in general. We're told over and over and over again nowadays that men and women are exactly the same. We have this notion that being equal must mean being identical. But even when we assert that men and women are created equal, equal does not mean identical.

Quick thought exercise: Be the empiricist, materialist Darwinist I asked you to be when thinking about the nature of sex in chapter four. You there? Great. Now as that Darwinist, look at a man and a woman. Are they identical? Nope. OK. Now look at other animals. Do we note generalized differences of behavior traits in males and in females that seem to have somehow a relationship to their physical differences? We do? Almost universally? Even in situations where species have the ability to change sex in a single-sex environment, they only do that because there are distinct differences amongst the sexes and they need the complementarity of those traits? OK, good to know. Thought experiment over.

It is worth noting a further point that G. K. Chesterton makes: The idea of equality, even of men amongst men and women amongst women, is patently false from an evolutionary perspective, and must appeal to God, to being *created* equal. Chesterton says, "The Declaration of Independence dogmatically bases all rights on the fact that God created all men equal; and it is right; for if they were not created equal, they were certainly evolved unequal." If you look around, you'll see that if we base all rights on "survival of the fittest," equality plays no role whatso- ever — for example, some people are more fit than others. But if we know that God created all humans with equal dignity, then poor or rich, strong or weak, tall or short, athletic or not, female or male, we are alike at least in dignity, if not in other measures! The point in all of this is simply to make sure we understand that men and women are different. *Different.* So we can't say, "Me be- ing friends with a girl is no different than me being friends with a guy!" That just doesn't take reality into account. It *is* different. You might assert that the differences don't matter, and we will get there, but it is categorically different.

Back when I was in college and wondering why the same romantic-feeling interference kept happening, and I was ponder- ing whether it could ever *not* be that way, my friend Kevin said, "Dude, the thing is, your body knows there's always a possibili- ty." And at the most basic level, that is one difference that affects male-female relationships. Your body knows what your brain might deny; that since you are of opposite sex and genetically dissimilar (which means they are *not*, in fact, like your brother or sister), there could be a sexual connection there. That gives your friendship a different tone, and one that potential or actual romantic partners pick up.

This was the real-deal conversation I had with myself. So if any of this is like, "Hey man! I'm not ignoring basic biology and reason here, you are," my response can only be, "Yup. I sure did do that. But you and I don't have to do that any longer, so let's not, shall we?" Let's keep moving together, with an acknowledgment of physical reality in place. We come to the idea of "platonic" cuddling, spooning, kissing, maybe making out here and there, occasionally having sex. Here I'm just going to keep staring at our hypothetical individual making this claim until it gets really uncomfortable — and if it seems wild or unfathomable to you that such a person exists in reality, I promise I have had this conversation with real human beings. Multiple real human beings. If you are one of those real human beings, I apologize for how uncomfortable this conversation probably is — you don't do any of these things with platonic friends of the same sex,[2] so what would make you characterize those actions as platonic when done with someone of the opposite sex? It's exactly because there is a difference between the two. If we're honest with ourselves, that physical contact, affection, intimacy appeals to us because there's validation, there are the sensations of love in that contact. Someone compatible loves us, and loves us enough to touch us, be close to us, and let us know we are lovable. That feels good, and it's easy to think that that meets a lot of our needs. But if it doesn't reflect an actually intimate relationship, that's a problem. And if it *does* reflect an intimate relationship, then it ought to be a romantic relationship, or not exist at all. Neither you nor your best friend should have to live in a limbo of intimacy unfulfilled.

"But what's the matter with being best friends? We're not *doing* anything." Now look, I'm not saying men and women can't be friends at all. What I'm saying is that being best friends, or even really close friends, is problematic. Because then, even if we say, "We're not *doing* anything," we're wrong. Sharing the intimacy of your heart with someone of the opposite sex (or honestly, with anyone) is not nothing — it's a major something. Emotional intimacy is a prerogative of best friends, of close friends, but most of all, of a husband or a wife. It's worth noting here that if you're unmarried and you get married, the level of intimacy in your other relationships (even with close friends of your same gender) will change as well. Every other relationship except your relationship with God must be secondary to your relationship with your

---

[2] OK, I'll grant that through cultural or personal habit, some platonic friends of the same sex do kiss, but we're talking about general rules here.

spouse because you are called to share fullest intimacy, emotional and otherwise, with them and them alone. It's part and parcel of making a free, *full*, faithful, fruitful gift of self. It's the counterpart to why sex outside of marriage is wrong (or actually, isn't even really sex [cf. chapter 4]). Between men and women, deep intimacy is *meant to be* both spiritual and physical. So if you have one without the other, or you're in a state in life where one or the other would be inappropriate, you need to fix that. That might mean stopping one-on-one hangouts, might mean dialing back the depth of conversation, or in some circumstances, it might even mean walking away from one friendship to protect the most important friendship in your life. Your husband or wife deserves the fullness of your person, and you can't possibly have the deeply loving, self-sacrificing intimacy that you desire with your true love if that intimacy is on loan to someone else.

"But I'm not married now! I'm not even dating anyone. I need to be heard and understood by *someone!*" That might very well be true, but then we're called to find that with a friend of the same sex. If we try to put the duties of hearing and understanding on someone of the opposite sex, they become our emotional placeholders. We *use* them for the emotional intimacy we gain. It bears repeating that this is categorically different because of our sexual complementarity. Certainly it is possible to emotionally use someone of the same sex too, to set them up as a rival against our beloved (or future beloved), to talk to them about our relationship problems instead of taking it to the person we're actually in a relationship with! And that's not good. Any use of another person is bad, but it adds another element of use and of rivalry when we (consciously or unconsciously) gain the additional validation of sexual complementarity. Remember, the opposite of love isn't hate, it's use. Use takes the gift of self and turns it into selfishness. It doesn't give you or the other person the opportunity to really make a full gift of self to anyone else, like, for instance, a someone else who desires to truly make a gift of themselves in return. That's the other part of the issue. If you continue to use someone as an emotional placeholder (which is bad enough in itself), eventually they become an emotional place*taker*. You won't be able to fully connect with romantic partners, because your heart is divided. And this can get really bad.

I knew a woman (let's call her Jane) who married a guy (let's call him Dick) who for years had been best friends with another woman (let's call her NotJane). Dick stayed best friends with NotJane even after Dick and Jane got married. Dick's wife was not his best friend, NotJane was. He still hung out with her one-on-one (because things just weren't "the same" if his Jane was there too), he fully admitted that there were things that he would tell NotJane that he didn't tell Jane (and he explained this to Jane as though there wasn't an ounce of weirdness about that), and he would call NotJane his best friend. Out and about, people assumed Dick and NotJane were married and that Jane was some third wheel. Dick had spent years developing closeness and intimacy with NotJane, but not with Jane. Jane and Dick both said that even when he was off alone with NotJane, they never had sex or anything, they were just really good friends, and liked spending time together. We all believed that. I still believe it! And I still think it was wrong and weird as hell. Eventually Jane realized that when she wanted to share emotionally with someone, her husband wasn't there for her. And he never shared his emotional life with her; why would he? He had NotJane. Dick and Jane were married, they had sex and stuff, but Dick's heart was somewhere else. After many tries to win him over, including therapy (which Dick complained about and commiserated about with NotJane), Jane finally left, heartbroken. Dick didn't really seem to notice.

So where does all of this leave us? If we want to love our friends, and we want to love our spouses (or future spouses), we should be friendly with our friends, but give our hearts only to our husband or wife. After all, it's the promise of the husband and wife to love as Christ loves, and bring their beloved to the Father. If we love that way, then in our full gift of self, we find that our restless hearts rest in God.

SO NOW WHAT?

- Want to have your main relationship forever be a platonic bestie? Cool! Then develop a lot of emotional intimacy with someone you have no romantic interest in (or at least they have none in you). If you ever get into a relationship, still rely more on your bestie because you've known them longer and bros before, um, you know, ladyfriends.

- Or, if you want to have friends AND a full, free, faithful, fruitful relationship with one other person, don't place expectations of intimacy on another. If you're married or in a serious relationship headed towards marriage, that means addressing issues or concerns with your partner first, and confiding in them, rather than in a (frequently quite well-meaning) rival. If you're unmarried, that means confiding in God, and in those people (family, close friends) that he has placed in your life and on the same path as you. But don't develop close relationships with people who could even possibly be romantic partners unless you enter into a romantic relationship with them, in which case, see above.

- Ask yourself: What am I doing to uphold the dignity of my friends and myself? Am I an encouragement toward virtue or an occasion of sin? How do I help my friends preserve their most important relationships and preserve themselves for relationship? What can I do better? One tip here: If you find yourself going, "I think I need to take a step back from X opposite-sex platonic-but-too-intimate relationship," generally the best solution is not to schedule a one-on-one time to have a long, intimate conversation about how you need to dial back your intimate conversations and stop seeing each other one-on-one. I don't know if that sounds obvious or counterintuitive, but I can tell you from experience that it doesn't do either of you any favors. My thought back at the time was, "Well, I owe X that!" But the truth was, it just kicked the can of protracted, inappropriate intimacy down the road, instead of just taking the necessary step back.

6

Supercharge Your Career, Supercharge Your Life!

(How we're missing our vocation)

"Go ahead, be evil. Do you need a social mission? Hell, no. Profit is the mission."

— *Inc. Magazine*, "Why Shark Tank's Kevin O'Leary Wants You to Be Evil"[1]

"[Work] is a bond of union with others, the way to support one's family, a means of aiding in the improvement of the society in which we live and in the progress of all humanity ... [but] for all that, you should put your professional interests in their place: they are only a means to an end; they can never

---

[1] Bill Saporito, "Why Shark Tank's Kevin O'Leary Wants You to Be Evil," *Inc. Magazine*, March, 2016, https://www.inc.com/magazine/201603/bill-saporito/shark-tank-kevin-oleary-be-evil.html.

be regarded — in any way — as if they were the basic thing."

— St. Josemaría Escrivá, *Christ is Passing By*

How do you measure a person's value? Or your own self-worth? Does it come down to "net worth?" We say things like, "Elon Musk is worth $68 billion! He's worth more than Warren Buffet now." Does it come down to career? As children we don't talk about what job we want to do, but about what we want to *be*. "I want to *be* a firefighter." "I want to *be* an actor." "I want to *be* a billionaire." Does it come down to our definition of success?

Maybe it's some combination of the three. We're all familiar with the stories of people for whom achieving career success justifies any means, be they lying, cheating, or white-collar crime. Nowadays, we may think of Billy "Fyre Festival" McFarland, Bernie Madoff, or Gordon Gekko (to use a fictional example). But this isn't a new phenomenon. From Ponzi to Machiavelli to Richard III to Zaccheus the tax collector to Haman the Agagite, as long as there have been means of achieving success and power, there have been those willing to abuse them. "Oh come on," you might be saying, "I know none of the stuff they did will make me happy, even if it did make me successful! I mean, how did those people live with themselves? I'd never do that!" And you'd probably be right. Most of us won't be tempted to use murder, geopolitical manipulation, or massive financial fraud to achieve our career goals. However, the desire to choose expediency over integrity plagues all of us. We don't frequently confront the option to sell our soul for all the kingdoms of the world. We do, however, frequently confront the option of committing peccadilloes to earn an extra dollar, save face with the boss, or keep a little more back on our taxes. I've worked a number of jobs in my life, in a number of fields, and look back with regret on some of the choices I've made (and since confessed). I've bolstered a job title on a resume; I've misrepresented myself to encourage a customer to make a buying decision on my timeline; I've made up answers to questions I didn't know the real answer to. When we do these things, they don't just hurt the people we're dealing with, they hurt us ... and not just when we get caught! When we choose expediency over integrity, we're saying that some thing, big or small, is worth more than our honesty and honor, more than our relationships, more than our soul, more than ourselves. And placing more importance in some potential gain rather than in our own person is somehow remarkably not great for our sense of self-worth.

That's one way we can tie our self-worth to our careers, which actually ends up sacrificing our self-worth to career advancement. We might, however, take a different perspective. Perhaps I say to myself, "I certainly won't do that! I vow to be scrupulously honest and upright in all my business dealings ... but yeah, I still do want to make as much money as possible, drive a nice car, have a great house, you know, and then give the rest to charity. The more money I make, the more good I can do, right?" Well, perhaps in some ways that's true; there are plenty of people who have behaved honorably, had a lot of career success, and done a lot of good with their influence. Great career success coupled with great integrity can create great benefactors, good investors, and inspiring teachers on a macro scale. Many churches would never have been built, many works of art never made, many charitable endeavors never executed, many missions never undertaken, without the generosity of those who worked hard to make them possible. Should we all be impoverished, think small, or skip work to go to daily Mass because "God first?" No, but if we look at work goals as the gauge of our success in life, we have the wrong focus.

"But wait!" you say, "My work *is* the important thing! I'm a social worker!" or "I'm a therapist!" or "I'm a firefighter!" Some of our jobs may be as far from the Machiavellian end of the spectrum as possible (although simply practicing any of these professions doesn't incontrovertibly guarantee freedom from selfishness, pride, or other human vices). Some of us want to use our careers to influence others and change the world. That's great, but there's still an issue here. Let me illustrate.

A friend of mine and I once got into a long conversation about life, careers, and relationships. Like me, he's an actor and writer. As we were chatting about matters on the relationship front, I inquired of him when or if he planned on asking his girlfriend (whom he'd been seeing for quite some time) to marry him. He replied that that wasn't on the immediate horizon, and I asked why not. He explained that God had placed on his heart an intense call to change the world through the art he would make. That he had a story, a script that he had to write, produce, and bring to fruition, that would inspire, influence, and affect the next generation. "I've got to pursue this. I've got to do this before I can move forward with my relationship. This is a call from God, my art is my vocation!"

OK, press pause. Have you ever said something like this? Or had a friend who did? Does it sound a little similar at all to your six-year-old self wanting to grow up to be your career? The truth is, we are not our careers, and while our careers might involve God calling us, they are not our most important calling from God. Your career may be art, it may be charity, it may enable you to do great good, but it's not your vocation. As Saint Josemaría Escrivá points out in the quote at the beginning of this chapter, while the work we do can provide many occasions for good, it remains the means to an end. It may be a good thing, but it is not *the* thing.

What, then, is *the* thing? What is our vocation (which, as you may know, comes from the Latin for "calling")? The Catechism says "By his reason, man recognizes the voice of God, which urges him 'to do what is good and avoid what is evil.'" (*CCC* 1706) It speaks of our "vocation to beatitude" (*CCC* 1716) to blessed life. And by blessed life, I don't mean "#blessed," which indicates how everything's going our way right now and we want to brag but also hide the fact that we're bragging. "Just got a raise at work! #blessed, #grateful, #hardestworkerintheroom." "Vocation to beatitude" means that our life is blessed (read: *holy*) because it is a life united to God. It is God's beatific nature and our sharing in his beatific life that in turn makes our lives blessed. The Beatitudes certainly don't indicate a life where "everything's going my way," but they do indicate a life united to God. They bear repeating here:

> Blessed are the poor in spirit, for theirs is the kingdom of heaven.
> Blessed are those who mourn, for they shall be comforted.
> Blessed are the meek, for they shall inherit the earth.
> Blessed are those who hunger and thirst for righteousness, for they shall be satisfied.
> Blessed are the merciful, for they shall obtain mercy.
> Blessed are the pure in heart, for they shall see God.
> Blessed are the peacemakers, for they will be called children of God.
> Blessed are those who are persecuted for righteousness' sake, for theirs is the kingdom of heaven.
> Blessed are you when men revile you and persecute you and utter all kinds of evil against you falsely on my account. Rejoice and be glad, for your reward is great in heaven, for so men persecuted the prophets who were before you. (Matthew 5:3–12)

Mourning? Meekness? Persecution? Being reviled? These are

not qualities and states of life that we would generally consider "#blessed." When we think of our jobs, how many of us (even those who work in charitable fields) can truly say that our work itself meets these demands? None of us, in fact, because these aren't demands that our jobs can meet. These aren't demands that are put on work at all: They're demands put on us. This isn't a question of what work we do, but who we are in our work. Our vocation, our calling, is to holiness, to blessed life. The Church says that some of us will live out that calling in married life: Becoming meek, a peacemaker, and merciful with our spouses and our children. Some of us will live out the call to holiness, to purity of heart, to mourning, to being persecuted, in the priesthood or the religious life. But whether we're called to marriage, the priesthood, religious life, or none of the above, we are *all* called to a life lived out of love for God and neighbor.

Back to the story of my conversation with my friend. What was wrong with his desire, or at least with his action plan? The desire to do good, to show beauty and truth, and to effect change certainly wasn't the problem. And it might very well have been God tugging on his heart; I'm willing to believe that was highly possible. The problem arises in the ranking and priority he gave to it. He was willing to indefinitely delay what might be his true vocation (i.e., the call to lay down his life in marriage), for the sake of this other pursuit that ought to have been subservient. And that, I think, actually serves as an excellent metric for career goals: Does *fill-in-the-blank* in your career serve your vocation? Does this *fill-in-the-blank* act as a means to the end of holiness, or does it detract from it? If you are called to marriage, does your work support and serve your family or take you away from your family? If you're called to the priesthood or religious life, does the work you're doing, the *stuff* of your day, truly serve your sacred spouse?

Right now in my life, my wife and I have been taking a hard

look at this. We've been asking ourselves if it really makes sense to make so many of our life choices based on our careers. I've lived in Los Angeles and have been acting professionally for the last decade; she's been here and in this career pretty much her whole life. But we're starting to ask, "Gosh, does this place and this industry contribute to us growing in holiness and happiness? Or does it detract from it? Does this career need to be our focus? Or would we be holier, healthier, happier, and more whole if we reprioritized?" We're pretty emphatically discerning that we need a shift. We're realizing that maybe our unspoken thoughts of career as calling don't quite hold water.

You see, when my friend said that his art was his calling, he voiced something I had often thought myself. In that context, however, I realized we both were wrong. Perhaps not wrong entirely (Pope Saint John Paul II's "Letter to Artists" gives great hope to all who struggle to live as creators in the image of God), but wrong in execution. I replied to him, "If they show my demo reel at my funeral, I've made a terrible mistake in my life. If my greatest contribution to the world is the roles that I've played and the work that I've done, that's actually a depressing thought." If I make the next *Citizen Kane* (or whatever great movie you'd prefer to imagine here), but I neglect truly loving my wife and raising up children to God, what good have I really done? Or worse yet, what if I spend my whole life trying to make the next *Lawrence of Arabia* with the same consequence of neglect, and I *don't* manage to achieve a blockbuster classic? Then I've neglected my calling from God to love as he loves, in favor of a subservient calling at which I also failed! I would rather do *all* things with an eye toward my true vocation, to put all things "in their place," rather than miss my vocation chasing my art (or my career). Again, no matter my work, my art, and whether or not I make the next blockbuster, if my coworkers see Christ in me (not in the work I do, but in who I am at work), if my wife loves Christ all the more in loving me, and if my children meet Christ through me (not because I worked so hard for a charity, but because I showed them so much charity), I will have lived my vocation. If not, I won't have.

"Ah but hold on!" you might say, "I'm not neglecting my kids and my wife/husband! I'm not even married yet!" Or "Look, I have to work and pay off my debts before I enter the seminary/ convent!" Or, "I'm not delaying getting married, I just haven't met the right person yet. I haven't met my 'vocation'!" Or maybe simply, "I don't have a lot of other stuff going on right now and my work gives me purpose!" But all of these miss the point a little. Your work doesn't give you purpose, God gives you purpose. He lets you share that purpose with others through your work … *and through the actions and interactions in the rest of your life.* This is where all these above things we might say about our current state in life are missing the point as well: Our primary vocation is the call to holiness. I remember early in my post-college life complaining about how it was so hard to "not be in my vocation." I thought things would be easier when I got married (or became a priest, if it happened to be one of the days I was sure that was my vocation), just as soon as I was out of this limbo, this waiting game. But the truth is that I never really was in a waiting game. I needn't have felt like I was waiting for my vocation, or even like I was waiting for my career. I had no need to wait to be holy, to seek good, to practice the beatitudes. I had my calling from day one — I was born into my vocation. God called me to holiness from the moment he created me, and he gave me my marching orders in baptizing me priest, prophet, and king. And he has done the same for you. The real question is: What are you waiting for?

We've talked in past chapters (and will more in future chapters) about reorienting our focus in our relationships with others. But here the point is to remember what our true calling is, what our true job is, no matter what career we might have. So, whether or not you're a billionaire CEO, whether or not you discover a cure for cancer, whether or not you successfully teach multiplication tables to first graders, you can be merciful, seek righteousness, be pure of heart and poor in spirit. Know where true satisfaction comes from, where true success comes from. Your first job is to "love the Lord your God with all your heart, and with all your soul, and with all your strength, and with all your mind," and job two is like it: Love your neighbor, spouse, children, and even your enemy, as yourself (cf. Lk 10:27). Then, no matter what career you're in, or work you're doing, you can be holy, and live a life that is truly #blessed.

SO NOW WHAT?

- Are you ready to supercharge your life? Well, literally the only thing you have to do is supercharge your career! So plot out exactly the fastest course to do that, do whatever it takes, ruin as many people's lives as you have to, so long as you can make a name for yourself.
- Or, if you want to put your professional interests in their place, as Saint Josemaría Escrivá might say, run a little inventory. How can you be the person who uses work as a bond of union with others? How can your career support your family rather than undermining it? (Remember, if we're brothers and sisters in Christ, you certainly don't need to be married or have kids to support your family.) How can you use your work and live out your work life as means of aiding in the improvement of the society in which we live, and in the progress of all humanity? Progress of all humanity, no big deal, right?

Take some time with this, and let it be an occasion to look less at your career, and more at who you are in your career.

- Finally, ask yourself, "What am I waiting for?" Then stop waiting, and start doing the work that God is calling you to do … because you can start living your vocation today.

7

Live Longer, Do More, Get More!

(Our obsession with quantity over quality)

"Yes, indeed, it's good to be rich in old age. According to a new study, wealthy men and women don't only live longer, they also get eight to nine more healthy years after 50 than the poorest individuals in the United States and in England."

— *The New York Times*, "Rich people don't just live longer. They get more healthy years."[1]

"Our labor here is brief, but the reward is eternal. Do not be disturbed by the clamor of the world, which passes like a shadow. Do not let false delights of a deceptive world deceive you."
— St. Clare of Assisi

---

[1] Heather Murphy, "Rich People Don't Just Live Longer. They Also Get More Healthy Years," *New York Times*, January 16, 2020, https://www.nytimes.com/2020/01/16/science/rich-people-longer-life-study.html.

Have you seen *Pirates of the Caribbean: Dead Man's Chest* (the second one)? A lot of stuff happens. Like, a lot. The romantic leads get arrested at their wedding and we meet about a million new characters (most of whom are covered in undersea life because, as everyone knows, Davy Jones isn't just a figure of speech, he's an immortal, undead squidhead who honest-to-goodness collects the souls of shipwrecked sailors, and is in fact often materially involved in their shipwrecking; so you better watch out). Everybody runs from cannibals, we meet a voodoo enchantress, our favorite characters make shockingly selfish decisions tantamount to mass manslaughter, everybody starts racing to find Davy Jones' heart (which is not on his person), there's some more gross negligence, and the movie ends unresolved. But not to worry, at least we know that of all the people the Kraken consumed, Jack Sparrow is the only one that our heroes can possibly *care enough about* to bother saving from a fate worse than death. Lost yet? Yep, me too.

It was a long movie.

I also thought it was one of the worst movies I'd ever seen. Now, you don't have to agree with me (maybe you hate the third one more), but my point is that just as a movie being longer doesn't make it better, we're frequently so focused on living longer and doing more that we neglect living better and doing good.

Why are Wal-Mart, Amazon, and Costco the top three retailers in the world?[2] I, for one, have 1-quart Ziploc bags to last me until the year 2030, and more baking soda and turmeric than I may ever use (odd shopping list, I know), all because I get so excited about getting so much more so cheaply. How many news segments, Instagram accounts, books, TV shows, and celebrity personalities are dedicated to trying to live longer and do more?

---

[2] Cally Russell, "Who Are The 10 Biggest Retailers In The World?," *Forbes*, January 9, 2020, https://www.forbes.com/sites/callyrussell/2020/01/09/who-are-the-10-biggest-retailers-in-the-world/#5b096d0b3802.

Even many that claim to be about living better really only actually mean living longer or being more productive. A longer life free of medical issues and more full of stuff? That's about the best life that we can hope for, if we listen to the "breakthroughs" on the nightly news, or the fitness/keto/vegan/paleo/billionaire/"boss inspo" on Instagram, or the self-help books that are so popular they have to be ranked separately than other nonfiction by the New York Times Bestseller list. In the metaphysically-musing TV comedy *The Good Place*, Ted Danson's supernatural character Michael ponders humanity's preferential love of frozen yogurt over ice cream. "There's something so human about taking something great and ruining it a little so you can have more of it," he reflects. Herein lies the question that we forget (or ignore) over and over again in our obsession with quantity over quality: What value is more of something if it isn't better? Who cares if we have more crap? Like we talked about in chapter 3, the more stuff I have, the more I keep discovering that it doesn't satisfy me. I get things I want and only think, "OK, got that, now what?" Who cares if we *do* more? If they play my demo reel at my funeral, or I've spent my whole life with the busyness of cleanliness and healthiness and scientific learning all for nothing to happen, who cares? What was it all for? What is the point of a long life if its main selling point is simply its duration? *Pirates of the Caribbean 2: Dead Man's Chest*: super-long, tons of stuff happens, none of it matters.

This plays out in an odd and upsetting way in our culture. According to the American Foundation for Suicide Prevention, middle-aged and older adults consistently have higher suicide rates than younger groups, with those aged 85+ occupying the #1 or #2 spot for suicide rate in all but one of the last eighteen years.[3] The reasons behind this are undoubtedly complex, from loss and

---

[3] https://afsp.org/suicide-statistics/.

loneliness, to suffering and illness, to the loss of a sense of purpose. No matter the reason, the stats clue us in to a startling reality: As our lives go on longer and longer, we stop prizing length of life for its own sake. When Americans reach retirement, the question of whether doing more and having more satisfies us stops being theoretical, and becomes practical. We finally have a moment to stop and think, instead of being in work mode day in and day out. And when we do stop and think, what do we conclude? Well, as one late-middle-aged man put it: "Vanity of vanities! All is vanity. ... All things are full of weariness; a man cannot utter it. ... I have seen everything that is done under the sun; and behold, all is vanity and a striving after wind" (Eccl 1:2, 8, 14).

The writer of Ecclesiastes calls himself Qoheleth (the Teacher). But because he talks so much about how he sought wisdom, and had everything under the sun and denied himself no pleasure as the king of Jerusalem, he is generally thought to be King Solomon.

> I said to myself, "Come now, I will make a test of pleasure; enjoy yourself ... I made great works; I built houses and planted vineyards for myself; I made myself gardens and parks, and planted in them all kinds of fruit trees. I made myself pools from which to water the forest of growing trees. I bought male and female slaves, and had slaves who were born in my house; I also had great possessions of herds and flocks, more than any who had been before me in Jerusalem. I also gathered for myself silver and gold and the treasure of kings and of the provinces; I got singers, both men and women, and delights of the flesh, and many concubines. (Ecclesiastes 2:1, 4–8)

I thought Mark Wahlberg's 30,000-square-foot French palace-inspired mansion with a wine cellar, home theater, gym, giant pool, and two-story library was pretty crazy. But Solomon? He made himself entire parks for his palace! He didn't just have pools for swimming and Marco Polo games, he had pools just to water the *forest in his garden!* He had herds and flocks like Ted Turner. He had other kings and rich guys paying him a cut of everything they made, and performers at his beck and call like Dr. Dre. He had servants, slaves, and prostitutes like … nope, never mind, I'm not going to try to figure out a modern comparison for that part. In any case, Solomon had everything he could think up, did anything and everything he wanted to do, and lived to a ripe old age, doing and having it all pretty much the whole time. And yet, looking back on all of it, he says it's all vanity, and the only feeling he can muster about it all is weariness. He lived longer, did more, got more, and his only response is a despairing, "Oh no … is that it?" He had a long life filled with goods, but found himself questioning if his life had been any good.

You might be thinking, "Wow, that's nice and depressing, Kaiser, thanks a whole lot! I mean, Solomon basically sounds suicidal even though he had everything he ever wanted, so where does that leave me?" Good question. I was recently in confession with a priest who knew about the work I've done on various Catholic projects and my writing. And after I finished telling him my sins, he said to me, "When you spend a lot of your time doing good work, work for the Church, stuff like that, you have to remember that that's not the same thing as being good, as living a good life. Doing good things still isn't sufficient to make us good … and truly *being* good is what really matters." Bottom line: You can't "make up" for sin; you can't trick your soul into being fulfilled; you can't trick God into thinking you love him. "This people draw near with their mouth and honor me with their lips, while their hearts are far from me" (Is 29:13). The underlying message from the priest was that there was a big part of my heart that was just in all this for me, and I was keeping that part of my heart far from God. That's why, as I admitted in chapter 3, I'm often not satisfied with what I'm doing in my life, and it all seems to be "vanity and chasing after wind," to quote our wearied biblical friend. So, if sheer quantity, whether of stuff, of experiences, or years, can't make us happy or fulfilled, and even "doing good things" doesn't necessarily satisfy us in our lives, what does? Living for God.

That's the good news in all this: While following the cultural wisdom of quantity, of accumulation, is an endless exercise in futility, we can immediately change our entire experience of life if we refuse to buy into that. When we spend our time living for ourselves, we soon find that "The drink would not satisfy, food turned to ash in our mouths, and all the pleasurable company in the world could not slake our lust" (That's from the *Pirates of the Caribbean* — the first one which is pretty OK!). But if instead of living for ourselves, we live for God, suddenly the quality of every action in our lives becomes good. Everything we have becomes a blessing we can give thanks for, and even our trials and sufferings take on the triumph of heroism. It reminds me of Chesterton's meditations on the difference between martyrdom and suicide in "The Flag of the World" and "The Paradoxes of Christianity" chapters of *Orthodoxy,* respectively:

> A martyr is a man who cares so much for something outside him, that he forgets his own personal life. A suicide is a man who cares so little for anything outside him, that he wants to see the last of everything. One wants something to begin: the other wants everything to end. In other words, the martyr is noble, exactly because ... he confesses this ultimate link with life; he sets his heart outside himself: he dies that something may live. The suicide is ignoble because he has not this link

with being: he is a mere destroyer; spiritually, he destroys the universe.

No philosopher, I fancy, has ever expressed this romantic riddle with adequate lucidity, and I certainly have not done so. But Christianity has done more: it has marked the limits of it in the awful graves of the suicide and the hero, showing the distance between him who dies for the sake of living and him who dies for the sake of dying.

That difference in understanding life and our purpose in it is what makes the difference between despair and joy, between the suicide and the martyr, between Solomon and a saint.

For instance, there's a vast difference of perspective between that weary king of Israel, and the young Blessed Chiara Badano. If you're not familiar with her story, Chiara was what some people call an "everyday saint." She wasn't a nun, didn't spend fifty years caring for the poor, and didn't perform any miracles during her lifetime. She was just a regular girl with regular interests and regular problems. She liked sports, music, and dancing; she struggled a little in school and sometimes got made fun of; but this regular girl with a regular life is on her way to sainthood right now because of how she loved Jesus and wanted to live her life for him. "I want to choose Him as my only spouse. I want to be ready to welcome Him when He comes. To prefer Him above all else."[4] When she was sixteen, she found out she had a rare, painful form of bone cancer called osteogenic sarcoma. That diagnosis quickly saw her enter the hospital for an extensive treatment process. Throughout her whole time in the hospital, everyone marveled at her joy. Her doctor, Antonio Del-

---

[4] Ann Ball, *Young Face of Holiness: Modern Saints in Photos and Words* (Huntington: Our Sunday Visitor, 2004).

ogu, said, "Through her smile, and through her eyes full of light, she showed us that death doesn't exist; only life exists."[5] And a friend who visited her in the hospital said, "At first, we thought we'd visit her to keep her spirits up, but very soon we understood that, in fact, we were the ones who needed her. Her life was like a magnet drawing us to her." She took walks with another patient at the hospital struggling with depression, even though walking became very painful for her. But when asked about her pain, she simply said, "There's only one thing I can do now: to offer my suffering to Jesus, because I want to share as much as possible in His sufferings on the cross."

Contrast Solomon's reactions to Blessed Chiara's. Solomon thinks on all the big stuff he did, and all the sweet swag he got, and says, "I considered all that my hands had done and the toil I had spent in doing it, and behold, all was vanity and a striving after wind, and there was nothing to be gained under the sun" (Eccl 2:11). Chiara donated her savings to a friend doing mission work and said, "I don't need this money any more. I have everything." Solomon looks at everything he has, and all the ways to spend his time and says, "All things are full of weariness, a man cannot utter it" (Eccl 1:8). When encouraged to stop walking with the depressed patient and get some rest for her own wearied bones, Chiara said with peace, "I'll be able to sleep later on."[6] Solomon sees that everybody dies, thinks that's unfair to the wise (like him) and responds by straight up hating life, "For of the wise man as of the fool there is no enduring remembrance, seeing that in the days to come all will have been long forgotten. How the wise man dies just like the fool! So I hated life, because what is done under the sun was grievous to me." (Eccl 2:16–17). When Chiara found that she had no hope of remission, she react-

---

[5] Chiara Luce Badano, Focolare Movement, Focolare.org/en/ January 30, 2012.
[6] Colleen Swain, *Ablaze: Stories of Daring Teen Saints* (Missouri: Liguori Publications, 2011).

ed not only by loving life, but joyfully accepting her death, "Don't shed any tears for me. I'm going to Jesus. At my funeral, I don't want people crying, but singing with all their hearts." Despite everything he had, Solomon found no joy. Blessed Chiara Badano had the joy of living for Christ, and in that, found she had everything. She died three weeks before her 19th birthday, and showed everyone around her that a life needn't be long to be great.

One final time of picking on poor Solomon to close out this chapter. He said, "[T]he eye is not satisfied with seeing, nor the ear filled with hearing" (Eccl 1:8). Perhaps though, he could be satisfied if he changed his focus; and so could we. If we love God first, and desire God first, then our entire perspective and experience changes to one of the quality of love, instead of disappointment in the quantity of pleasures. Then we might say together with Saint Paul, "What no eye has seen, nor ear heard, nor the heart of man conceived, what God has prepared for those who love him" (1 Cor 2:9). This isn't a question about how many great things we get if we love God, but an affirmation that if we love God, every aspect of our lives becomes great.

SO NOW WHAT?

- He who dies with the most toys wins, right? So do whatever you can to acquire more and live longer! Then you'll be, well, the winner! (Happiness not guaranteed.)
- Or, what if rather than living longer and doing more, you'd prefer to live better and do good? Start by contemplating your perspective on possessions, finances, and comfort. What place do they hold in your life? I remember hearing a story that Frank Sinatra loved watches, and he knew that he had a tendency to really enjoy his possessions, watches es-

pecially. So (according to the story), if someone ever complimented his watch, he would take it off and give it to them, because he wanted to very forcefully remind himself to be detached from his possessions. Now, I'm not trying to hold up Ol' Blue Eyes as a paragon of virtue, but he provides us with an example of great self-awareness when it comes to the stuff he had. How can you take this and apply it to all those places in your life that tend toward accumulation, possession, and "having," rather than creation, devotion, and giving? How does this apply to your relationships, your career, and your next Ikea run?

- Do you want to be more like Solomon Qoheleth or more like Chiara Badano? What perspective shift would it take to see everything as blessing? To see everything as an occasion for joy? To see even pain and death as consolation and life? How do you love God above all things and love your neighbor as yourself? How can *you* do all of this, *today*?

You Won't Believe This Amazing Wedding!

(Marriage isn't an end in itself ... and
a wedding certainly isn't)

"Ultimately, your wedding day is about celebrating the love between you and the person you're about to marry. But there's another goal at hand: Throwing one seriously epic party that your guests will talk about for years to come."

— Brides Magazine, "20 Ways to Throw the Best Wedding Ever"[1]

"It takes three to make love, not two: you, your spouse, and God. Without God people only succeed in bringing out the worst in one another. Lovers who have nothing else to do but love each other soon find there is nothing

---

[1] Gabriella Rello, "20 Ways to Throw the Best Wedding Ever," *Brides*, October 7, 2019, https://www.brides.com/gallery/tips-for-planning-the-best-wedding.

else. Without a central loyalty, life is unfinished."
— Venerable Fulton Sheen, *Three to Get Married*

We make a big deal about weddings in our culture. Sometimes we even make a big deal about marriage. But no matter which one we're busily idealizing and idolizing, most of us end up looking at both wrongly. I've known a lot of women who have been compiling ideas for what they think will be their perfect wedding since high school (or even middle school). They just needed to find a guy to show up for it. They had Pinterest boards for their dress, and more for the bridesmaid dresses; knew the picture-perfect church, and an even better reception venue; had floral #inspo for days, and had selected the exact Pantone colors for every garland, invitation, and placecard. They'd spent years preparing for a wedding, but almost no time preparing for marriage. It's like preparing for a graduation party without ever having studied.

At a Catholic Engaged Encounter (a marriage preparation weekend required by many dioceses), they emphasize over and over, "A wedding is a day, a marriage is a lifetime." The wedding is there to celebrate the beginning of a lifetime commitment, a covenant of two entire lives promised daily to each other; but instead of letting the wedding be a "bon voyage" moment, we've tried to make it an end in itself. Why are celebrity weddings often televised events? We watch weeks of coverage leading up to the wedding day, coverage that sometimes eclipses in duration the marriage itself (Kim Kardashian and Kris Humphries come to mind). But celebrity weddings aren't the only crazy ones. A headline in *The Onion* joked, "Man and Woman Get Drunk, Blow $30,000 in One Night," because, guess what: The average cost for a wedding in the United States by 2020 was $30,433, *before* the cost of the honeymoon, and in some cities like New York, averaged over $70,000.[2]

We've made the incidental an idol, and the integral has become inconsequential. The celebration of the commitment becomes somehow more important than the commitment it celebrates ... which should be a clear sign to us that something is out of order. And it's easy to see that that's true. The question of divorce rates is a complicated one, one that doesn't really fit the adage we frequently hear that half of all marriages end in divorce. The truth is much more finessed, with factors including demographics; whether a given marriage is a first, second, third, or further marriage; whether a marriage ends in separation; and the fact that fewer people are even entering into marriage in the first place. However, certainly we all have people in our lives who've gone through divorce, we all know more people cohabiting than our parents knew, and we all know people who complain about their marriages and their spouses.

Is it any wonder? Really? After all, how can we possibly do well at something we haven't actually prepared for at all? If you never trained for a marathon, what are the odds you'd finish? Even if you did finish, what are the odds you'd love and enjoy the marathon you didn't train for? Very low, as I'm sure you'd conclude. I've run long distances without having trained, and I can tell you that the resulting shin splints and stress fracture were no fun at all. And now to share a much bigger confession than poor running habits: I've made marriage an idol and paid the price. I never spent months or years fantasizing about the perfect wedding, but I did spend months and years imagining the perfect marriage without adequately discerning or preparing for it. I fell into the second half of that initial equation I posited: I made a big deal not about a wedding, but about marriage. I made marriage

[2] John B., "Average Cost of a Wedding 2020," *WeddingStats.org*, February 5, 2020, https://www.weddingstats.org/average-cost-of-a-wedding/.

the goal. Unfortunately, marriage isn't the goal or the finish line — it's the starting line!

Have you known men and women who are eager to just "get married and settle down," who "can't wait to find the right person to share the rest of my life with," who just "want someone to say good night and good morning to, you know? Oh, and have sex with?" Or are you that man or woman who is eager and can't wait, and just want all these things? Now the problem isn't exactly that any of these are wrong in and of themselves; they're just woefully incomplete! The problem is that all of that stuff simply isn't what marriage is! Marriage isn't "settling down;" it's taking up the cross of truly living for the good of another. It isn't "sharing the rest of my life with someone;" it's learning to live a new life that is not your own. It isn't saying good night and good morning and having good sex; it's becoming good in every moment, that you may help your spouse and your children see clearly the good of heaven and the good of God.

At my cousin's wedding, the priest giving the homily said something provocative, almost scandalous, which elicited a collective gasp from the attendees. He said to both my cousin and his bride, "You will be the primary instrument of your spouse's crucifixion." The words fell hard on an audience expecting to hear oft-repeated platitudes of how wonderful marriage is, how this should be "the happiest day of your life," and maybe assorted jokes about the differences between men and women meant to make everyone shake their heads with a chuckle and ponder what folly conflict is. Instead, this priest had the audacity to say that this young husband and wife would be the principal instrument of each other's crucifixion! What would a celibate priest know about the relationship of husband and wife? Well, as it turns out, a lot. Because while most husbands and wives intimately know only their own, and perhaps their parents' relationships, as the witness for the Church to marriage, the priest at least somewhat intimately knows the relationships of dozens, if not hundreds, of couples. And as one whose vocation called him to be married to the Church, he also knows experientially the joys and trials that a married couple goes through, which in Ephesians 5, Saint Paul likens to the love of Christ for the Church. This priest knew that it is the bride who draws forth from the husband love, generosity, self-sacrifice, courage. And it is the husband who draws forth from the wife love, gentleness, support, strength. None of these most important virtues happen in a vacuum; none of them are ones you can simply exercise on your own. You can only fully exercise them in relationship.

We all must be crucified if we hope to experience resurrection. We have the choice of how to respond to the cross: resist or embrace. We know that Christ embraced his cross. Think of what that fully means: The cross of Christ is the sins of the world, the sins of the very people he has come to save and to love — you and me. We, his bride, responded to this saving love (and so often continue to respond) with apathy, impatience, choosing ourselves over him, fear, bad faith. … And yet, even as it kills him, even as we cry "Crucify him!" he embraces us all the more. We fight against God and sin against the one who lays down his very life to save us; yet he embraces us tighter. So Saint Paul can write to Christian spouses in Ephesians 5:21–22, 25: "Be subject to one another out of reverence for Christ. Wives, be subject to your husbands as to the Lord. … Husbands, love your wives, as Christ loved the Church and gave himself up for her," because we are each other's crucifixion — but also each other's resurrection.

The priest went on to say that our role as cross to our spouse is not an invitation to wound, nor an admonition to endure abuse, but a call to be an instrument of grace. Love is patient when the choice of patience or impatience lies before you and you choose patience. Love is kind when you choose to be kind to your spouse. Love does not brood over injury when you eagerly forgive your spouse after he/she hurts you. Love hopes in all things and endures all things because that is the choice you make. And in so doing, you and your spouse embrace each other, and love each other — even while you are sinners — into the perfection of heaven (cf. 1 Cor 13:4–7). That, at least, is what happens when we embrace this opportunity to grow in goodness, love, and self-sacrifice. When we embrace the cross, we find the yoke easy and the burden light (Mt 11:30).

If, however, we reject the cross, marriage becomes a yoke indeed, and not an easy one. As I mentioned, I made marriage an idol; one where I thought could take a selfish and destructive relationship and make it good. Spoiler alert: That doesn't end up actually being a marriage. I had met a woman who "checked all the boxes," so to speak — she was Catholic, pretty, and intelligent — and I was going to make it work. Unfortunately, she didn't love me (but I checked all the boxes too), and at best I only loved the idea of the person I thought I could make her become. Sound unhealthy yet? Both of us figured we were just fine the way we were and didn't need to change; but change we did, and for the worse. I had a knack for judging all of her choices and opinions, moral or otherwise, as indicators of moral deficiency, and she responded by doubling down on them to assert her independence. Judgment turned to insults, insults to conflicts we refused to resolve, and unresolved conflicts to deep, abiding resentment. Still we kept on, got engaged, and she moved two thousand miles away hoping absence would make the heart grow fonder. Yes, this all sounds crazy now, and would have sounded crazy then if I had just looked at it honestly. I got more judgmental and jealous apart from her; she said sometimes it was only the invitations having been sent out and the nonrefundable deposit on the reception hall that kept her going through with the wedding. The list goes on, and doesn't get any better. We had a wedding. People came. We were distracted enough by a party to construe our feelings as something approaching happiness for about eight hours. Then we settled into all the same resentment, anger, and jealousies from before, only now heightened by the idea that we couldn't get out of it. "Ah, but marriage is supposed to be hard! Suffering is good!" I told myself. I don't know what she told herself, because she wasn't open with me and I didn't want to ask.

The truth is, marriage may be challenging, but it should always be a challenge faced as a team, two people together as one, up against the world, who would do any good thing for the other's good. It shouldn't be a challenge because you have values diametrically opposed to one another; are actively mean, demeaning, disrespectful, or cruel to each other; engage in jealousy or give cause for jealousy. That is not a relationship that wedding vows can fix, because they clearly aren't vows that are meant. Saying you promise to love, honor, and obey doesn't work if you have no intent to do such a thing. And boy did that become clear in our case. After three and a half years of this mess, of seeking advice and not implementing it, of refusing to let go, forgive, and start anew, we separated and divorced, and I petitioned the Church to examine the case for an annulment (meaning the Church examines to see if a real, valid marriage ever really existed in the first place, or if some essential element was missing).

The separation and divorce were just about the most painful six months of my life. The year-and-a-half-long annulment process, while still painful, became one of the most grace-filled experiences of my life. If you've suffered divorce, I encourage you to go through the Church's annulment process, and really dive into what the Church asks of you. The Church asked both her and me separately to describe our relationship, from beginning to wedding to divorce, in deep, probing questions that were uncomfortable and heartbreaking, but forced us to be honest with ourselves in ways I think neither one of us had been. The Church asked witnesses who had known us from the beginning to do the same, and expected the same unvarnished honesty from them. After all of it, the Church gave us the opportunity to read every piece of testimony: mine, hers, our witnesses'. I went into the archdiocesan offices one afternoon. The nun handling our case handed me the testimony, and I sat in a room for the next several hours reading it. I asked the nun afterwards, and she said that only about 10 percent of the people involved in annulments elect to read the testimony. But in my own experience, that's what changed my entire perspective of this whole relationship, and revealed what went wrong. Sure, it was unpleasant to read and relive the vivid illustrations of the worst parts of our time together; but seeing the honest experience that she went through, as well as what our friends had seen from the outside and had never felt able to say, and even rereading what I had written, opened my eyes to a deep understanding. I understood far better who I was as a person, who she was as a person, how both of us had approached relationships in the past, how we had approached this one, and most importantly, how I could approach relationships in the future, if the Church did grant the annulment.

There's one extra interesting point: This great perspective shift, this reckoning and change in self-awareness, all happened before I even knew whether or not the Church would find a case for nullity. Sometimes the problems in a relationship are not defects that actually prevent a marriage, and no case for an annulment is found. I don't know what that would be like to live through, and if you've suffered divorce, that may be a question on your mind, something keeping you from asking the Church to look at your marriage at all: "What if they do look at it and say that I'm still actually married?" I can only tell you that during the two years it took for the Church to issue a verdict, my heart had changed enough that I was ready to accept and live out whatever the verdict was. Through the annulment process, I stopped seeing marriage as an idol that would fix my life and give sense to my suffering. Instead I learned to see marriage as a great challenge that God might be asking me to take on, or a great good that God might be asking me to give up in order to better serve him.

During this time I had one of the few (maybe only two) profound spiritual experiences I've had in my life. I was praying — well, more like railing against God — asking why, if I had tried so hard to do the right thing, why I was going through this terrible suffering, this awful marriage breakdown. Suddenly I experienced a vision (which, as I say, I am not prone to, and generally have to fight rolling my eyes if someone else talks about having one. Not defending that response …). I saw Christ carrying his cross, and felt (more than heard) him say, "Because I want to share this intimate part of myself with you." In one moment, my whole understanding of the world, my place in it, and my suffering all flipped upside down. "God, this isn't fair, I'm being rejected by the bride I tried to love!" *I saw the Bride of Christ, his people, crucifying him, and yet he embraces the cross, he embraces them … me.* "God, why would you let me suffer like this?" *I see in his eyes that this suffering is the only way I can experience the suffering of God, and the love he has that overcomes that suffering.*

Suffering isn't good because we can offer it up, or because "that which doesn't kill me makes me stronger." Suffering is good because if we embrace it, it actually improves our intimacy with God and enables us to love. Why? Because that's why God became man: to suffer, and to suffer not so that he could understand us, but so that we could understand him; the God who would endure anything for us because he loves us first (cf. 1 Jn 4). And that's what marriage is: A daily laying down of our own lives to better live one life of love with and for our spouse. That's what the marriage tribunal found had never been present in my relationship. After reviewing all the testimony, it became clear to the Church that on the day of our wedding, one or both of us had not meant our vows (and likely not on most of the other days of our relationship either). We hadn't really intended to give up our own self-interest and live for the good of the other, we hadn't intended to hope all things and endure all things side by side, because we were so rarely side by side, but usually on different sides. We never intended to embrace each other, or embrace the cross. It was, unfortunately, only going through this experience that opened my eyes to all of this; to my own selfishness, my pettiness, my shortcomings, and to the issues on her side of the equation as well. So while I still regret a lot of the things I did and decisions I made from the beginning to the end of that relationship, I also rejoice in the opening of my eyes that God brought out of it. I saw very clearly the ways that I needed to be a better person, and a better person in relationship, the opportunities to love as Christ loves.

As I began to date again, instead of just glossing over red flags, I saw more clearly the words and actions that would lead to the same situation again; the indicators that we were not on the same page or the same team, that our hopes and desires for life were opposed to one another. It made for a number of interactions that didn't get past a second date ... or even a first. But I realized that that was a mercy too: It was better to figure things out quickly rather than bump along in a relationship that wouldn't really go anywhere. I was learning to stop treating the incidental (having similar likes and dislikes, loving to hang out, laughing a lot — "she 'checks all the boxes'") as important, and to start treating the integral (i.e., the things that are most important in life: God, holiness, love, and heaven — these are the things she wants the most too!) as essential. And in doing so, I found love, true self-sacrificing love, with a woman who, though we had a lot of incidental differences, I knew I could trust to love me, and I knew I would truly mean my vow to love her. I could say with Adam, "This at last is bone of my bones and flesh of my flesh" (Gn 2:23). So, we had a wedding, got married, had a baby, and have another on the way, and we daily pick up our cross (admittedly some days better than others), embrace each other, and walk together with the grace of God.

If you want to be miserable and alone, stay in a relationship where you're both out for yourself, and consistently just have to endure one another. But if you'd rather not be, then find a relationship where you both consistently submit to one another out of reverence for Christ; a relationship where you love and respect each other as Christ loves the Church, and where you both truly live the life of the one that is greater than two.

SO NOW WHAT?

- An epic wedding sets you up for an epic marriage, so focus on getting that right! Then, whenever you have problems, you can be like, "Look, we already sunk $50k into this marriage on our wedding day, so we're gonna make this work!" Talk about motivation!
- Or, if you'd rather live a marriage of mutual love and respect, focus on being a pair who are both cross and resurrection. Whether you're married, dating, or neither, you can (and really must) start with yourself. How can you be the kind of person you'd like to be married to? How can you honor and respect and be on the same side as your beloved (even if you're not sure who your beloved is yet)? If you're single or dating, what can you do to hold that ideal, that common worldview, as essential, and let the incidentals fall to the side?
- I remember hearing Mother Miriam (I'm 99 percent sure it was her) relate one instance of spiritual

direction she had given. A woman was complaining about her husband, how their love had dissipated over time, and how they barely endured each other now. Mother Miriam told her to stop thinking of love as a feeling, and start thinking of it as action — actions taken to show deep caring and respect for her husband, even when (actually, especially when) she didn't feel it. Be giving, kind, compassionate, supportive in all things, verbally offer and ask forgiveness, and be on her husband's side (the only exception being if he was actively encouraging her to sin). The woman came back some weeks later and told Mother Miriam that her marriage was transformed. After being so lovingly cared for and respected and encouraged by her, the woman's husband asked her where this change had come from. She replied that she hadn't been loving him well, and that she wanted to change that. And far from the response of "Yer darn right you haven't! Finally you've got some sense in you," that she might have expected, her husband realized that he too had not been loving her well, and sought to change. Now, it doesn't always work so quickly. Indeed, if it's to be truly loving, there can't be the condition of it "working" at all. But this approach takes you out of the trap of "romantic chicken" (a term from Catholic psychotherapist Dr. Gregory Popçak). Instead of holding back to see who will be loving first, instead of saying, "Well, I would be more kind if he would be more generous," or "I would clean up after myself if she ever did any work," you have the opportunity to be good and live out love regardless of the outcome. If you're married, how might you begin to implement this more in your married life? If you're in a dating relationship, how can you live this out better in your discernment process? And if you're still seeking a relationship, how can you be a more loving person, that a like-minded and like-living individual will recognize that common bond with you?

9

These Celebrity Babies Have It All!

(How we've turned children into accessories and obligations)

"Celebrity babies are definitely some of the most famous babies in the world. History has presented the world with a number of memorable babies such as the first test-tube baby but let's face it, with parents like Prince William, Kim Kardashian, Beyoncé, these babies are bound to be more famous and massively popular while making news headlines and magazine covers."

— Just Richest, "10 Most Famous Celebrity Babies in the World"[1]

"The so-called right to abortion has pitted mothers against their children and women against men. It has sown

---

[1] Amara Onuh, "10 Most Famous Celebrity Babies in the World," *Just Richest*, August 7, 2013, https://justrichest.com/celebrity-babies/.

*violence and discord at the heart of the most intimate
human relationships. It has aggravated the derogation
of the father's role in an increasingly fatherless society.
It has portrayed the greatest of gifts — a child — as a
competitor, an intrusion and an inconvenience."*

— Saint Teresa of Calcutta

As a culture, we're obsessed with babies. People go crazy over celebrity babies. TMZ somehow got a hold of Kim and Kanye's baby's birth certificate and less than twenty-four hours after the happy event, gleefully broke the news that North West had been born. Brad and Angelina sold the first photos of their daughter Shiloh for charity, for the amount of $4.1 million, and a further $5million to $7 million for later licensing. Mark Kurschner, a senior VP at Wire Image, said that celebrities routinely sold exclusive photos and licensing, and that prices were going through the roof.[2] When Beyoncé revealed she was pregnant with twins, her post became the most liked ever on Instagram (at the time) a mere seven hours after posting.

Some people do a lot to acquire kids, and I don't mean adoption. From intense fertility treatments and surgeries, to artificial insemination, to in-vitro fertilization, where up to fifteen or so embryos are created in the hopes of implanting one or two (93 percent of embryos are never implanted, and almost half of all IVF embryos ever created have been thrown away[3]), to paying men for sperm collected through masturbation, paying women to have surgery to have eggs harvested and sold, to putting it all

---

[2] Julie Day, "Brad and Angelina Sell Baby Pics for Charity," *The Guardian*, June 6, 2006, https://www.theguardian.com/media/2006/jun/06/pressandpublishing.marketingandpr.

[3] Steven Doughty, "1.7 Million Embryos Created for IVF Have Been Thrown Away, and Just 7 Per Cent Lead to Pregnancy," *The Daily Mail*, December 30, 2012, https://www.dailymail.co.uk/news/article-2255107/1-7-million-embryos-created-IVF-thrown-away-just-7-cent-lead-pregnancy.html

together in surrogacy, babies are now frequently created in a laborious process that, from the outside, sometimes appears more akin to building one's preferred Mercedes model than receiving the natural result of the love of a husband and wife.

And yet, one out of every four babies is aborted each year.[4]

Do any of these things seem strange when taken all together? It strikes me that a society that clamors to see the first pictures of celebrity babies, and at the same time rails that abortion is a human right, has something terribly wrong. I promise this will not just be the "abortion chapter," but the fact that we see something remarkable, marvelous, beautiful, and yet disposable in children is a horrifying proof that our culture treats children as objects and accessories.

Living in LA and being in the entertainment industry, I see some of the more glaring examples show up very close to home. Both Michelle Williams in her speech at the Golden Globes and Busy Phillips in her speech on the Supreme Court steps explicitly said that their abortions allowed them to become the successes they are today; and that now, when the time is right for them, they have children on their own terms. Or what about the myriad other stories of celebrities and the well-to-do having babies "on their terms"? Because paid surrogacy can be very prone to taking advantage of low-income women, it's banned in many countries and several US states — or at least highly regulated. But California has some of the most paid-surrogacy-friendly laws in the nation (some authors even calling the laws "lax"[5]). So around here, it's not uncommon to purchase eggs from one

---

[4] Special tabulations of updated data from Sedgh G., et al., "Abortion Incidence Between 1990 and 2014: Global, Regional, and Subregional Levels and Trends," *Lancet*, 2016, 388(10041): 258–267. Accessed on Guttmacher Institute website. https://www.guttmacher.org/fact-sheet/induced -abortion-worldwide.

[5] Mark P. Trolice, MD, FACOG, FACS, FACE, Álvarez, Natalia, and Fernandez, Sandra, "Surrogacy in the USA – Is It Legal in All 50 States?," Babygest, October 18, 2019, https://babygest.com/en/ united-states/.

woman and pay a different woman (often with children of her own to care for) to carry the resulting children as a surrogate. Unfortunately, bearing children genetically unrelated to you carries a much higher risk than a normal pregnancy. This can lead to serious consequences, including miscarriage, loss of a full-term child, and permanent health issues or even death for the surrogate mother. How many people have to be treated as objects for these children-on-demand to happen? One woman is seen as valuable only for her eggs. Another woman is seen as valuable only for her womb and for having a financial situation that might dispose her to surrogacy. The children themselves are bought and paid for. As opposed to situations where people are paid for their work, surrogates are paid for themselves. We think the days of indentured servitude as long gone, but what else can you call it when people are selling their own bodies at a cost not measured in dollars, but in lives? All of this — all of this cost, all of this extraordinary effort — is made to have babies, but to have them on our own terms.

Now look, I don't bring this up to point a finger and go, "Isn't that horrible? Isn't that disgusting? Doesn't it just make your blood boil?" These are tragedies that people reframe in their own minds to be able to function in the rest of their lives (and they want everyone else to jump on board with their reframing too). But far from making these people unrelatable to me, or making me hate them, I rather find myself asking if I'm guilty of the same underlying issue. The issue is how we — whether married or single — think of babies; not just babies in general, but each and every individual baby, each and every incarnate soul. There are two ways of thinking. Do I see my baby (present or future) as some*thing* I have, or as some*one* to live and die for? If my baby is something I have, then at best they're an accessory, something I've decided to take on now when I feel it fits me and my life. Is this a pitfall you've fallen into? Is it a temptation you've noticed (or now notice) in your heart? Is it something you've heard in conversations with friends or family — this idea that kids should be put on hold until after we travel the world, after we become executives and make enough money to hire the nanny, after "We're ready?" Sometimes in a married relationship, there may in fact be "grave reasons" (as the *Catechism* phrases it) to defer pregnancy. But are any of the above reasons "grave?" At minimum here, a baby is seen as an obligation, a life occupier, something for me to alternately love and resent depending on how the rest of my life, my other obligations, and my manifold priorities are all presently shaking out. At worst, this baby becomes a burden, a reminder of regretted choices or events we'd rather forget, and the only thought is to cut it out of our lives.

If instead, we know in our minds, hearts, bodies, and souls that a baby isn't something we have, but rather someone to love with our whole lives, everything changes. Love may be a challenge, but it needn't be a burden. "For my yoke is easy, and my burden is light" (Mt 11:30). A *person* isn't just a life occupier, or an obligation: A person is an immortal soul in whose presence we are privileged enough to stand. As C. S. Lewis points out in *The Weight of Glory*:

> It is a serious thing to live in a society of possible gods and goddesses, to remember that the dullest most uninteresting person you can talk to may one day be a creature which, if you saw it now, you would be strongly tempted to worship, or else a horror and a corruption such as you now meet, if at all, only in a nightmare. All day long we are, in some degree helping each other to one or the other of these destinations. It is in the light of these overwhelming possibilities, it is with the awe and the circumspection proper to them, that we should conduct all of our dealings with one another, all friendships,

all loves, all play, all politics. There are no ordinary people. You have never talked to a mere mortal. Nations,
cultures, arts, civilizations — these are mortal, and their
life is to ours as the life of a gnat. But it is immortals
whom we joke with, work with, marry, snub, and exploit
— immortal horrors or everlasting splendors.

That's what a person is. Babies, children, while you can dress them
in cute clothes and carry them around slung over your shoulder
(OK, maybe better not to) aren't accessories; they're marvels. And
we've all been one, yet that shouldn't make it any less marvelous.
Rather, the marvelousness of children should remind us of the
awesome dignity of every human around us. And if we lose the
wonder of children, we have lost wonder indeed. It's this sense of
awe and reverence that G. K. Chesterton suggests so separates a
proper sense of children from the disposable idolatry we commit
and that I've been railing against. In his essay *A Defence of Baby
Worship* (which, again, is different from idolatry), he says:

> The essential rectitude of our view of children lies in
> the fact that we feel them and their ways to be super-
> natural while, for some mysterious reason, we do not
> feel ourselves or our own ways to be supernatural. The
> very smallness of children makes it possible to regard
> them as marvels; we seem to be dealing with a new race,
> only to be seen through a microscope. I doubt if anyone
> of any tenderness or imagination can see the hand of
> a child and not be a little frightened of it. It is awful to
> think of the essential human energy moving so tiny a
> thing; it is like imagining that human nature could live
> in the wing of a butterfly or the leaf of a tree. When we
> look upon lives so human and yet so small, we feel as if
> we ourselves were enlarged to an embarrassing bigness

of stature. We feel the same kind of obligation to these creatures that a deity might feel if he had created something that he could not understand.

My wife points out that if we let them, children teach parents unfathomable things about our own relationship to God, which is kind of the point of this chapter. Not in the sense of "don't kids say the darnedest things?" or "Ha! Out of the mouths of babes!" but in the sense that we should learn to parent our children the way that God our Father parents us. How we treat babies ought to reflect (and improve) the way we treat all humans (like C. S. Lewis pointed out above), and lead us into a deeper relationship with God. If you have children, this can transform your relationship with them and attitude towards them. If you don't have children, and especially if you're single, you can still draw essential truths for your spiritual growth, as well as understand better this part of your vocation, if you're called to be a parent. I don't know how else to lay this out except in a "here are a few things I've learned" sort of way ... which I tend a little to rebel against for fear of it reading like a collection of shabby chic pallet-craft wall hangings from Etsy. But, oh well, here goes.

My daughter was created out of the love of her mother and myself. This baby is our love incarnate. How can I not love my love? If I want to love perfectly, how much must I cherish this love incarnate, this tiny immortal soul in my care? How much must God (who is perfect love) love me, and cherish me, and care for me?

God made us sharers in his act of creation. I have had one other vision than the one I recounted in the chapter on marriage (and again, I feel as weird saying this as I generally feel about other people telling me that they've had visions ...). It was around the same time, before I had even met my now wife. I saw myself and a wife in old age, gathered together with our children, their children, and several babies who might have been their children. We were inside, and yet above us stretched the stars and the whole universe, beautiful and terrifying and shocking in its immensity. And the universe was torn open slightly, in a gentle way, not a violent one, and my family stood in that cleft. And I was staggered by this realization of what I was seeing: that while God created all these lives, these incarnate souls standing with my wife and me, so had we. The only reason these people had come into existence was because God had shared his power of creation with us. This God, who made himself Father to me, created every single thing that is beautiful — the stars, the sky, the planets, sequoia trees, Zion Canyon, the endless waves of the ocean, toucans, peacocks, dolphins, whales, lions, leopards, coral reefs stretching for miles, rhinoceroses running on the Serengeti — and then turned to me and said, "Here. Now you try." That's who my daughter is: a beautiful creation that, through the grace of God, is a union of time and eternity. And that's who I am. And who my parents are. And their parents. I remember my dad teaching me to ride a bike (which, in my case, was a long and laborious process that he patiently stuck through), and how much he celebrated when finally I stayed upright on my own and rode circles around the elementary school parking lot on a Saturday. I think of my wife and me giving our daughter crayons, drawing a few things for her, showing her how they worked, and then handing them to her, "Here. Now you try." She scribbled and we thought it was the best thing anyone had ever done. If I can dote like that, how much does God, a perfectly loving Father, rejoice and celebrate when we live out the beauty and truth and love that we have learned from him?

Our daughter has had an interesting relationship with sleep. Now, most newborns, if you add up all the time they sleep, end up actually sleeping quite a bit. It's just rather inconveniently but evenly spread out in tiny chunks over a 12–24 hour period, depending on the baby. Thankfully, that didn't last long, and at seven weeks old, she started sleeping through the night. And then at four months, she decided again to sleep no more than 2 hours at a shot. When, at six months, she elected to switch to one hour sleep cycles before a fifteen minute screamfest of demanding to nurse, we were going absolutely insane and started to sleep-train (next baby, we're starting that ASAP, lesson learned). In any case, in some of those long, nearly sleepless nights from zero to seven weeks and four to six months, I had moments of epiphany while trying to calm my non-sleeping daughter. I knew (but she didn't), that she needed sleep, and that she was so upset because she was tired. I knew (but she didn't), that if she just calmed down, lay down, and closed her eyes, she'd feel better. I knew (but she didn't) that I knew what she needed, and if she'd just trust me and let me comfort her, her suffering would be lessened, we'd all be happier, and she'd be bursting with joyful energy in just a few more hours. And as I knew all those things that she didn't know about what was best for her, I (in the moments where I successfully cautioned myself to patience instead of utter breakdown out of exhaustion) pondered that perhaps this was the experience of God with me, sans the proximity to breakdown. How often in doing things "my way" — in sinning, in holding on to fear, in failing to love — are we crying babies? How much anxiety, frustration, anger, and despair do we experience simply because we ignore the God who is trying to speak quietly enough for us to stop and listen? That's how you get a baby to quiet down, right? If you yell, they'll scream; but if you whisper, sometimes at least they will quiet down to hear you. All this time that we spend resisting God, fighting God, ignoring God, our Father is holding us, trying to calm us, whispering, "Shh … my son, my daughter, listen. Trust me, listen to me. I'm trying to help you. Shh … shh … listen."

My daughter loves trying new things. She's not a timid child

— she went from walking at eleven months to running a month later. A couple months after that, if we heard any effort sounds that we didn't have eyes on, we ran to her, because she was invariably climbing up onto something that only mommy or daddy or gravity would get her down from. But if she hears a noise she doesn't expect and doesn't recognize, she's suddenly at our feet with her arms out, looking to be picked up instantly. And as soon as one of us is holding her, instead of concern or fear, she adopts a look of fascination, her eyes wide and tiny lips pursed as she points to the ostensible direction of the sound and utters a low, "Ooooo." Sometimes we even get to see that reaction without the brief fear precursor, when something provokes just the excitement; like when she hears a dog bark or sees a shiny car drive past. Then she's thrilled just to point and yell, "Mama, dada!" (and the word for whatever the thing is, if she knows it. She knows both "dog" and "car." That's right, we read *Go, Dog. Go!* No big deal). That's how I want to be with God. How about you? Don't we want that excitement, that trust, and that desire to bring everything to God? "God, did you see that? Did you see how great that was? Look, God, look!" We want to come to God when excitement isn't our prevailing response, too. "Yikes, God, that was unexpected! I want to be with you and I know that you'll bring me through it." My daughter wants mom and dad to be close while she's exploring this new universe. We're exploring this new universe too, and we want to be close to God while we do.

In seeing the things my daughter takes excitement and enjoyment in, I'm rediscovering the world anew along with her. She has loved seeing cats since she was four months old. And now, more than a year later, she still bursts out laughing every time she hears a cat meow. Or, if the cat doesn't meow, she'll make a meow sound for it, and then burst out laughing. Even if it's just a picture of a cat, or a bad drawing of a cat, she still meows, then thinks the meow is such a funny sound every time. Every. Time. Just about everything is exciting to her because it's new, and some things stay thrilling and hilarious no matter how many times they're repeated. She appreciates all the things she's never seen, and hasn't yet allowed repetition to dull her appreciation of repeated things. As Chesterton points out (again in *A Defense of Baby Worship*), "The fascination of children lies in this: that with each of them all things are remade, and the universe is put again upon its trial. ... Within every one of these heads there is a new universe, as new as it was on the seventh day of creation. In each of those orbs there is a new system of stars, new grass, new cities, a new sea." This is how I'd like to approach God and his creation: allowing new experiences and learning always to thrill. To realize, even in repetition, that there is always something to appreciate that I haven't before, something new I can notice about his creation that brings me closer to this God who is "ever ancient, ever new." Why instead do I cultivate a casual jadedness? "Oh yes, airplane travel is just the worst, I hate going to the airport ..." *To fly through the air like a bird, see the world miniaturize beneath me, and appear, like magic, on the other side of the country a few hours later!* "Ugh, the pollen floating around right now is getting dust on my car, and I have to take allergy medicine ..." *The pollen from these countless beautiful flowers blowing in this idyllic breeze and playing their part in the miracle of life.* "Blerg, how tedious it is to cook dinner every night, day-in and day-out ..." *To feed my family by participating in this art of creation, of taking raw ingredients and making a new, heretofore nonexistent dinner out of love for these souls in front of me.*

You get the idea. One other point about this thrill, this joy in both the new and in being able to perceive newness even in repetition (even monotony): Perhaps it reveals not just how we ought to be with God, but how God is with us. Christ tells us we must become like children if we wish to enter the kingdom of heaven (cf. Mt 18:3), and I'm sure a lot of that has to do with being docile, filled with gratitude, eager to sit at the feet of the master and learn to love as he does. But is it also conceivable that in God's supreme justice, unfailing purity, eternal joy and perfect innocence, there is something childlike? Or at least that the childlike reveal these perfections of God? I'll appeal one more time to Chesterton, writing in *Orthodoxy*, where he says:

> Because children have abounding vitality, because they are in spirit fierce and free, therefore they want things repeated and unchanged. They always say, "Do it again"; and the grown-up person does it again until he is nearly dead. For grown-up people are not strong enough to exult in monotony. But perhaps God is strong enough to exult in monotony. It is possible that God says every morning, "Do it again" to the sun; and every evening, "Do it again" to the moon. It may not be automatic necessity that makes all daisies alike; it may be that God makes every daisy separately, but has never got tired of making them. It may be that He has the eternal appetite of infancy; for we have sinned and grown old, and our Father is younger than we.

Whether or not you have children, you have opportunities each day to learn and grow as a child of God, and I pray that you'll seize those opportunities with grace. You can pray too that if you're given the gift of children, you'll ever love them for their own sake, as God does with you, and never treat them as an obligation or an accessory to your life, but instead as the great joy of your life. And you can pray to ever approach God with childlike confidence and love, to always be childlike with your Father, and never childish.

SO NOW WHAT?

- Babies — accessory or obligation? You decide!
- Or, if we want to recognize human dignity and respect the immortal souls around us, we need to rethink, reimagine, and re-experience our understanding of babies. Where do you fall into the trap of seeing children as obligation or burden? Do you ever simply see them as an accessory, something to obtain or possess, rather than to love?
- If you have kids yourself, in what ways are they revealing God to you, or revealing you to you, even if they don't know it?
- If you don't have kids, how can you take on Christ's teaching that "Unless you turn and become like children, you will never enter the kingdom of heaven" (Mt 18:3)?
- If you don't know if you want children/don't know if you can handle being a parent, might there be ways you are being called to grow in trust and humility in at least discerning a little further? How can you open yourself up a little more in reflection?

10

Time Hacks for Busy People!

(How our hectic schedules reveal our priority problems)

"When you're busy there's actually no time to be bored. That's because you're always around doing different things. Boredom just isn't one of them."

— Odyssey Online, "10 Reasons Why Keeping Yourself Busy is Good"[1]

"Idleness is the enemy of the soul; and therefore the brethren ought to be employed in manual labor at certain times, at others, in devout reading."

— Saint Benedict, The Rule of St. Benedict

---

[1] Vanessa Raffaele, "10 Reasons Why Keeping Yourself Busy Is Good," *Odyssey Online*, September 26, 2016, https://www.theodysseyonline.com/10-reasons-keeping-busy-good.

My friend Patrick (the amazingly talented singer-song-writer I mentioned earlier … seriously, Spotify this guy) is a self-admitted recovering ICanDoItAllAholic. Big project at work? "On it." Burger Tuesday get-together? "I'm there." Bar Trivia Wednesday? "You bet." Movie night Thursday? "Oh yeah!" Pick up a side gig to get finished on a tight deadline? "Try to stop me!" Hang out Friday, two get-togethers and a birthday party on Saturday? "Heck yes, I can do it all!" There used to be a running joke amongst all of our friends: "Is Patrick coming tonight?" "Yeah, he said he'd be here at seven, so I'm betting he'll roll in around 10:15!" Or if people were supposed to bring something to a party, only have Patrick bring an unnecessary item, something you could wait on, like a second dessert or an extra bottle of wine. If you needed ice or plates or napkins or anything, that wasn't going to happen on schedule. And Patrick knew it. One of his songs starts with the lyrics, "Well, I'm writing down this song about a quarter past last minute, / I always feel like there is more time." Even our parish priest picked up on it. One Sunday afternoon, Patrick showed up for Mass at about 4:10 p.m., and Father Tim said with surprise, "Patrick! You're early!"

Patrick, himself surprised, said, "Wait, early? Isn't Mass at 4:00?"

"No, 4:30," was Father Tim's reply.

"Oh … OK … I've got a thing at 6:00," said Patrick, as he got back into his car and drove to the church a mile up the road, arriving at 4:15 for the 4:00 p.m. Mass there.

Now, Patrick has gotten a lot better, since he's trying to not do this anymore. He commits himself a lot less, and has improved his scheduling and time management by leaps and bounds, but it took some major life events to wake him up to the need to slow down. And I don't think he's remotely alone in any of this. Heck, I take a (probably undue) grim satisfaction in saying "no" to most extracurricular commitments, and yet my wife, daughter, and I are routinely five minutes late to Mass, half an hour late for being fashionably late to social engagements, and five minutes late to our acting classes; all because we're trying to fit one more thing in beforehand, to run right down to the wire. So much to do, so little time.

And I judge that most people nowadays, especially in the United States, feel that way. How often, when asked "How are you?" do you reply, "Busy!" Or how often do you hear that reply? How often do we wear that as a badge of honor? But how are we really responding to this "so much" we "have to do," in this "so little time?" Instead of acknowledging that, yes it's true, time is fleeting and we should spend our time well, we just try to figure out how to fit more stuff into the same amount of time! Why are "hacks" so popular? Why is Amazon Prime destroying brick-and-mortar business? Why do we have meals shipped to us? Why do we microwave *everything*? Comedian Brian Regan points out that "They also have microwave directions for Pop Tarts … How long does it take to toast a Pop Tart? A minute and a half on the long side? There are people who don't have this kind of time? Listen, if you need to zap-fry your Pop-Tarts before you head out the door, you might want to loosen up your schedule." He might be right — maybe if ninety seconds is too long to spend cooking breakfast, the problem isn't the breakfast prep time: It's your overloaded day.

As a general concept, I agree with the adage that "Idle hands are the devil's workshop." But "keeping busy" isn't the solution. As Saint Benedict points out in the quote from his Rule that begins this chapter, we don't solve idleness by occupying our time, but by using time well! Busy isn't the opposite of idle, drive is. Going somewhere, making progress toward a definite end, that's the opposite of idle. We treat activity for its own sake as though it is somehow a good, rather than seeking intentional time spent well. And that's a further point: I have this idea that I'm just busy all the time, so busy, just gettin' stuff done left and right. But when I try to quantify *what* I've actually accomplished, I often draw a blank, or go, "Huh, yeah, I mean, that's a lot of stuff, but now in retrospect, I'm not sure it was really important stuff."

A couple months ago, I discovered the "Your Activity" tab in Instagram settings. If you use Instagram regularly, and haven't checked this, check it. It's downright scandalizing. The first time I checked it, I discovered that amidst my busyness, I was still somehow spending almost two hours a day on Instagram! What? That seemed crazy! But when I finally had it laid out there, I started paying attention, and realized, "That's my first instinct when I have what feels like a spare second: Grab my phone, check my email, and check Instagram." The more I paid attention, the more I realized I was letting that habit take my attention away from the actual important things I wanted to do: from my daughter, my wife, and my time with God. I was busy with nothing but distraction for two hours a day. I brought it to confession, and the priest suggested that instead of opening Instagram, I open iBreviary and pray. I made it for one week, then fell right back into my old habit. It's gotten better (this week I'm down to fourteen minutes a day, according to Instagram's "Your Activity" page), but still, what's going on here? I've got my priorities upside down! I'm treating time occupied as time well-spent, and in the end, I'm doing nothing. Even if your issue isn't Instagram and email, where could you still benefit by taking a really hard look and seeing if you're really spending your time in ways that matter, instead of just spending it. How often do we let ourselves get hypnotized by activity, rather than having a clear focus to cut through the noise?

In *Manalive* by G. K. Chesterton, the character Arthur Inglewood has a glimpse of the life he might live if he could just snap out of this hypnosis-by-busyness. He turns to the woman he loves but has always been too busy to pursue, and says, "That's the matter with all of us. We're too busy to wake up. ... There must be something to wake up to! All we do is preparations — your cleanliness, and my healthiness, and Warner's scientific appliances. We're always preparing for something — something that never comes off. I ventilate the house and you sweep the house, but what is going to HAPPEN in the house?" We're so busy doing, that we forget to stop and take stock of why we're doing what we're doing in the first place, and what we're supposed to be doing it for.

In Luke 10:38–42, Christ gently tells a very busy Martha that she's forgetting the *why* behind what she's doing. "Martha was distracted by much serving; and she went to him and said, 'Lord, do you not care that my sister has left me to serve along? Tell her then to help me.' But the Lord answered her, 'Martha, Martha, you are anxious and troubled about many things; one thing is needful. Mary has chosen the good portion, which shall not be taken away from her.'" Martha's busy doing things she thinks are necessary, but Jesus points out that she's forgetting the purpose of inviting him into her life in the first place — relationship with him. That's where our priorities should *start*.

I'm reminded of a conversation I've had multiple times with friends or acquaintances who say they were "raised Catholic." I ask them, "Where do you go to Mass now?" And more often than not, the response is something like, "Oh, man. Yeah. I'm just so busy now, I can't make it to Mass on Sunday. Like my weekends are packed. I literally can't fit it in." Let's get real here. Unless you're booked solid for thirty hours starting at 4:00 p.m. every Saturday through 10:00 p.m. every Sunday, you *can* technically make it to Mass. And if you're booked every Saturday afternoon through Sunday night, then you're not too busy to go to Mass, you're choosing to prioritize everything else over Mass. We get worried and distracted about many things, but there is need of only one thing. If we try to fit God in where we can, we'll find he doesn't fit anywhere, but if we "seek first the kingdom of God," we'll find a remarkable clarity defining what other things matter and how they fit.

Now maybe your challenge of seeking first the kingdom of God isn't a challenge in getting to Mass. Maybe you're struggling with making time for daily prayer, or for sleep and rest, or for intentionality and truly refreshing leisure. So how do you meet that challenge, that struggle? Well, start with a little self-knowledge. Take a hard, honest look at your life day-to-day, and see how and where you're spending your time. It may take several days of new awareness before you can really see it clearly (as I mentioned, it took me a week of checking my unconscious response to open Instagram before I really even started to be aware of it). When you do though, ask yourself if God is the starting point, or an afterthought. Honestly, even in prayer, I know I frequently focus just on "getting it done" rather than having it be time well spent with God. How about you? How do the activities of your day spring from or detract from your relationship with God? If you want to live with purpose, not just busyness, you have to remember your *true* purpose and make it your priority. "Seek first the kingdom" because where you spend your time, there your heart will be also (cf. Mt 6:21).

SO NOW WHAT?

- How are you? Keeping busy? Good for you! It means you're busy doing many things! Boredom just isn't one of them!
- Or, if you want to live with purpose and not just busyness, start with some self-reflection. Bring your awareness to every choice you make today and tomorrow (especially the unconscious ones). Write it down if you want. If you think you're spending a lot

of time on your phone, your computer, or a specific app, most of them now have usage data you can find (maybe under "Screen Time" or "Your Activity"). You might be shocked to find out exactly how much time it really is.

- Once you've sufficiently tracked and brought awareness to what you're doing with your time, ask yourself the following: How much of this activity brings me closer to God? How much of this activity brings me closer to friends, family, and the people God has placed in my life? How much of this activity brings me closer to a worthy goal? How much of this activity leads me to contemplation rather than distraction?

- When you've answered those four questions, there's only one more to answer, and it's a two-parter: How do I feel about that, and what do I want to do about it?

11

This Weird Trick Makes Everything Easy!

(Why we should be skeptical of "the easy way")

"Imagine your day-to-day life suddenly got a whole lot easier, and not because anything major changed. You still have your same job, friends, and family, but as if by magic — everything is simpler. Sounds good, right?! … So read on, and introduce a little coasting into your life."

— BestLife, "30 Genius Tricks That Will Make Your Life Easier"[1]

"Do not pray for easy lives; pray to be stronger people. Do not pray for tasks equal to your powers; pray for powers equal to your tasks."

— Blessed Solanus Casey

---

[1] Julia Malacoff, "30 Genius Tricks That Will Make Your Life Easier," *BestLife*, March 9, 2018, https://bestlifeonline.com/tricks-make-life-easier/.

There's a funny (albeit fairly foul-mouthed) sketch from College Humor that came out a few years back, called "Nicholas Cage's Agent." Nicholas Cage's agent is begging Nicholas Cage (well, a Nicholas Cage impersonator, obviously) to stop agreeing to so many terrible projects. After listing a few real movies, such as *Sorcerer's Apprentice, Knowing, Ghost Rider,* and *Wicker Man,* the agent tries to show Cage what he means by mentioning some other terrible offers that he should say no to … but Cage says yes instead.

"For example," the agent says, picking up a script, "you'd be playing a prisoner who asks if he can leave … and the warden says yes."

"And then I leave?"

"Yeah. That's it. Not a very interesting story. So this is the kind of picture you shouldn't be doing."

"I'm in!" Cage interrupts. And with that, the scene cuts to another day, after the box-office bomb *The Shawshank Exception* has come out.

Now obviously, as sketch comedy does, this takes a concept to an absurd place. But the concept is pretty revealing. We don't like easy stories. Why? Because, well, they're boring. "Tell me a story about the easiest thing you've ever done!" said no one ever. What stories do we like? We like stories that exemplify heroism, adventure, bravery, and romance (and I mean romance in the fullest sense, not cheap eroticism, but inspiration that moves our hearts). The fact is, while we may think we like things to be easy, we don't. This isn't to downplay the reality of suffering and difficulty we may experience in family dysfunction, crippling debt, underemployment or unemployment, sickness, or loneliness. The struggle is real, if I may use a trite phrase yet mean it sincerely. But is there a chance that these challenges are calls to growth? Are there ways that we can grow from our sufferings, and grow closer to God through them? Can our greatest triumphs, inspirations, and happiness come when we do things that are difficult, and do them with joy?

Our culture and our daily lives don't presently suffer from too much difficulty, but the difficulty of too much ease. In one of my favorite books as a child, Robert McCloskey's 1943 work *Homer Price*, young Homer's Uncle Ulysses is obsessed with labor-saving devices. To use our vocabulary, Ulysses is an "early-adopter." If it's automated, if it's intuitive, if it saves him from doing something manually, he wants it. But Homer notices that the more Uncle Ulysses becomes accustomed to ease, the more he also becomes impatient, lazy, less engaged in his work and his life. The easier things become, the less valuable they seem to us, and the less we're willing to work for them. We have knowledge at our fingertips, but we don't read past the headline, we don't listen past the soundbite, and we fall for more "fake news" today than we ever have. We no longer have to earn our bread by the sweat of our brows, and so we've stopped making food entirely; instead we pay restaurants to make our meals, PostMates and GrubHub to deliver them, and leave one-star reviews because it wasn't fast enough. Amazon promises us two-day delivery, so we lose our minds if it's delayed and we have to wait one more day. We … well, fill in the blank here with your experiences of desiring comfort and ease, and fill in the blank with your resentments when you experience anything less.

I remember being at a party once where two young women sat at the table in the middle of the room. There were people around them (including eligible guys) attempting to make conversation and engage with them, but they just buried their noses in Tinder, looking to make a connection with an eligible guy. Or perhaps, as they were eschewing contact with the humans in their midst, they were looking to fake a connection. Relationships are hard, Tinder is easy. Porn is easier. Why do 70 percent of men and 30 percent of women watch porn at least weekly? Why is 30 percent of the bandwidth on the internet used to transmit porn?[2] It's easier than making a gift of yourself to someone else. It doesn't ask anything of you. But does it satisfy? As someone who used to fall into that 70 percent of men, I can tell you it doesn't. Have you ever had an insect bite that itches like crazy? You scratch it, and you relieve the itch a little, but as soon as you stop, the itch feels worse. That's what porn does. That's what all easy things, all things that don't demand any sacrifice, do. They scratch an itch, but they don't relieve it. I remember a priest saying to me in confession, "Look, the impulse you're feeling and looking to fulfill is a *creative* impulse. Your body wants to participate in creation, and instead of satisfying that desire, pornography just makes it worse, because you don't get any closer to fulfilling any act of creation. You get no closer to making a gift of self. So when you feel that impulse, do something creative. Write, draw, make music, do something loving and kind for someone else, but create something. Let your desire to participate in God's creation, in making something out of nothing, in loving like he does … let that desire be fulfilled." And so that's what I started to do. Not perfectly, and I'm still not perfect, but thanks to the grace of God I haven't looked at pornography now in years. And my life is better, my mind is clearer, my heart is freer, my soul more creative, all from following that one small directive from the priest: Seek to sacrifice, to create, to love … in other words, don't take the easy way. Long before internet porn, long before Tinder, long before Amazon and Blue Apron and PostMates and a 24-hour news cycle, someone (Jesus) said, "Enter by the narrow gate; for the gate is wide and the way is easy, that leads to destruction, and those who enter by it are many" (Mt 7:13).

Now I'm not saying we should never go to restaurants, never

---

[2] "Survey Finds More Than 1 in 3 Women Watch Porn at Least Once a Week," *Fight The New Drug*, February 20, 2020, https://fightthenewdrug.org/survey-finds-one-in-three-women-watch-porn-at-least-once-a-week/.

order from Amazon, live on a subsistence farm, pump all our water out of wells, and never open a computer. I *am* saying that we should be skeptical of the easy way, very skeptical of choosing convenience as a way of life, and very conscious of how our choices and actions (easy or hard) affect our ability to live a life of virtue. Virtue opens up our ability to pursue the best things in life, rather than the pretty OK. As a quick check-in on that, we can ask ourselves, "What good things, what true things, what beautiful things are achieved, created, witnessed, or even appreciated without any degree of difficulty?" Conversely we can ask, "How does *being good* allow me to do good, appreciate the beautiful, and witness to the truth? Wouldn't I rather have *that* life than a just-so-so life (or worse yet, an evil life), denigrating the beautiful, and justifying lies to fit my lifestyle?" Now the whole point of virtue — "an habitual and firm disposition to do the good" (*CCC* 1803) — is to make it easy to choose the good; but it seems we much more often choose the easy instead of the good. How do we change that? We exercise discipline, sacrifice, and faithfulness in small matters so that we can exercise them in greater ones (cf. Lk 16:10). For me, that has meant literal exercise on a regular basis,[3] as well as disciplining my eating habits. It means setting time aside for prayer each day, picking up iBreviary instead of Instagram, and finding intentional ways to offer sacrifices out of love. A long time ago, my sister and I made Saint Thérèse's sacrifice beads. You might've heard of Saint Thérèse of Lisieux's "Little Way," which essentially consists of doing small things, small sacrifices, with great love. As a child, she used beads on a string to count up the acts of love she could do for God each day. Basically, it was a way for her to bring conscious attention to the moments where she was presented with an opportunity for sac-

---

[3] See my other book *Grit and Glory: Cross Training Your Body and Soul* (Huntington: Our Sunday Visitor, 2018) for more on that.

rifice, a choice between right or wrong, easy or sacrificial, small love or great love. If you too can find a way to bring that attention, that awareness to your life, and then make those choices for the good (or when it's a choice between goods, for the *best* good), you train yourself to prefer truth, beauty, goodness, and integrity above all lesser things.

Another time when I was in confession (boy, a lot of my stories involve me being in confession), I was talking to the priest about my problems with distraction in prayer and in my relationship with my wife and my daughter. The priest said, "OK, bring your awareness to that. When you're praying, when your mind wanders, bring it back. Don't beat yourself up, just be aware of it, acknowledge it, and bring your mind back to God. With your wife and your daughter, start by just not having your phone out when they're in the room. Put the phone away. If you become aware that you've got it out, or that you're not engaging with them, don't beat yourself up, just put distraction away and then listen. Make that sacrifice out of love." Again, it all starts with an awareness of our habits toward ease, toward lesser goods, and then moves to disciplining those, and then to actively choosing the best good, the sacrificial choice, the loving choice. When approaching ease (and honestly, when approaching sin), we tend to soothe ourselves by rhetorically asking, "I mean, c'mon, what's really wrong with XYZ? What harm could it do?" and then just not answering the question. We're much better off if we ask ourselves, "What *good* will XYZ do?" and then honestly answering it. If you can't come up with an inspiring answer, do something else. That question made a big difference for me in my battle with wasting time (and putting myself in the near occasion of sin) on Instagram. I so often asked, and didn't bother answering, "What harm could it do if I just pull up Instagram and browse a bit?" It wasted a ton of time, found me lingering on pictures that tempted me to lust or envy, and further disconnected me from the actual human beings in my life. But all that could have been avoided (and I do avoid it much more now) by asking myself, "What *good* do I hope to accomplish here?" Most of the time, an honest answer to that question would be, "Um, yeah, well, nothing, I guess." And so now I spend my time in ways that ask much more of me, but are much more satisfying than looking up bleary-eyed from an hour of Instagram rabbit hole-ing, feeling disconnected and useless. If that's not your experience, no problem. But ask yourself, "Where in my life do I ask, 'What harm could it do?' rather than, 'What *good* can I do?'" Where do you find yourself engaged in distraction rather than connection? Where can you choose to actively make a change to sacrifice out of love; to sacrifice momentary itch-scratching for truth, beauty, and goodness (and all without beating yourself up about it)?

Again, I'm not trying to downplay the suffering and anguish we can experience. I'm simply asking that we look at it from a different perspective. How does it look if we compare our suffering to the suffering and uncertainty of those in war-torn countries, utter and abject poverty, or not just dysfunctional but truly abusive relationships? How does it look if we let our suffering be a part of our lives that we are working through, rather than the defining characteristic of our lives? How does it look if we see our suffering as an opportunity for intimacy with God in the suffering of Jesus? How does it look if God is not only giving us a chance to conquer a difficult task and grow stronger, but to understand his sacrificial heart in the process? If we choose to challenge ourselves daily, to take up our cross and heed the call to love greatly, even in small things, we find ourselves far more fulfilled. Even more, we experience a new kind of ease: freedom. Freedom is the ease not of a life without sacrifice or of one that requires no effort, but of a life that embraces the effort and sacrifice with joy: the joy of knowing we're making choices with purpose, exercising that great human gift of free will, and through choosing sacrifice, growing in intimacy with our God of sacrificial love. In this sacrifice, we become more capable of loving and taking joy in the things we sacrifice for, and even in sacrifice and suffering itself. G. K. Chesterton captures this experiential change that comes from seeking sacrifice, from seeking virtue when he writes in the *Orthodoxy* chapter "The Ethics of Elfland:"

> [The aesthetes'] emotion never impressed me for an instant, for this reason, that it never occurred to them to pay for their pleasure in any sort of symbolic sacrifice. Men (I felt) might fast forty days for the sake of hearing a blackbird sing. Men might go through fire to find a cowslip. Yet these lovers of beauty could not even keep sober for the blackbird. They would not go through common Christian marriage by way of recompense to the cowslip. Surely one might pay for extraordinary joy in ordinary morals. Oscar Wilde said that sunsets were not valued because we could not pay for sunsets. But Oscar Wilde was wrong; we can pay for sunsets. We can pay for them by not being Oscar Wilde.

When we exercise our freedom to sacrifice out of love (to pay for sunsets, if you will), we discover that fulfilling joy that lets Christ tell us, "Take my yoke upon you, and learn from me … and you will find rest for your souls. For my yoke is easy, and my burden is light" (Mt 11:29–30).

SO NOW WHAT?

- Man, life's hard, right? Well, make it easy, bro! Do the minimum to get by, let yourself slack a little, flake a little, fake a little! You won't be happy, but life will be easy!

- Or, if you'd rather appreciate life and live a life worth appreciating, start by asking a couple questions. First, where is distraction robbing you of connection? Where is distraction a sign that you're letting the easy way pull you away from good and fulfilling things? How would your life look if you changed that? What do you need to do to change that? Hint: From my experience, going to confession is a great starting point, even if your "easy way" isn't particularly sinful. And finally, where are you really suffering in life, where are you really hurting, and how can you avoid it less and embrace it more in a healthy way? Again, even if it doesn't involve you sinning, confession's a great place to start. From there, do you need to write out and come to terms with your suffering? Do you need to "contend with God" like Jacob or Job, or like me railing against God about my marriage breakdown and divorce? Do you need professional counseling? Have the conversations, seek the help, acknowledge real suffering.

- Moving forward, what can you do to choose the freedom of sacrifice to live in truth, beauty, goodness, and joy? As I mentioned, I've found help in exercise, getting to bed on time, disciplining my eating habits, daily prayer, iBreviary instead of Instagram, sacrifice beads, and asking "What *good* can I choose?" instead of "What harm could it do?" It's worth noting, other than daily prayer, I'm not doing all of these every day. Some of them I probably should be, but we're sinners groaning together, remember? Find what works for you, and when you do, keep doing it, because it works, not because it's easy.

12
You're in Control!

(How to let go and let God in a healthy way)

"You can systematically conquer your anxieties and eliminate the external obstacles holding you back. You can take back control. Your life can be yours."

— Medium, "20 Ways to Take Control of Your Life"[1]

"Don't worry about me no matter what happens in this world. Nothing can happen to me that God doesn't want. And all that He wants, no matter how bad it may appear to us, is really for the best."

— St. Thomas More

---

[1] John Fawkes, "20 Ways to Take Control of Your Life," *Medium*, May 16, 2017, https://medium.com/@johnfawkes/20-ways-to-take-control-of-your-life-a7892bb66765.

"Just livin' that #bosslife!"

"If it's to be, it's up to me!"

"If I want something, it might not happen, but if I will it, it will happen!"

I once had someone really say that last one to me, out loud, in person. I realized he wasn't joking, and I think my diaphragm muscles are still recovering from the strain of suppressing my laughter just in time.

We humans have an obsession with being in control. Now, there's great good in true leadership and accountability, but that's not what we get all excited over. Allow me to illustrate. I went ahead and typed in #bosslife on Instagram, and didn't see pictures of heroic individuals (who've stepped up "like a boss," if you will), didn't see even inspiration from titans of industry or business magnates. What's pictured in the most #bosslife-y of posts? Fat stacks, sweet pads, pimped rides, and outrageous guns. Guns on money, guns on cars, guns on their own chairs. Know what the top "related hashtags" are that Instagram suggests I might also be interested in? #moneyteam, #rich, #millionaire, #millionairetoys, #luxurylifestyle, #billionairesclub, #richandfamous. Now, I'm not saying this is some empirical study on human psychology, but I think it still does reveal something true and interesting and convicting about us. When we picture a life to aspire to, when we picture leadership and the life of a leader, we picture money and power. No #bosslife picture shows a guy struggling to keep his eyes open at the end of a ninety-hour week while his employees party through the weekend. We don't see the boss who takes responsibility for her entire team, who demands much from her teammates, but more from herself. We see only images of these things that we think give us control, great ability to have things my way: money and power. If I have money up to my eyeballs, I can buy whatever I want (and just look at these pictures of houses, cars, and boats that prove it), and if I have crazy guns,

I've got the power to take anything else I want or stop anyone from taking it from me. I think of Frank Sinatra's most popular song of all time, "My Way." The first time I heard it, I thought, "Wow, what a tragic, heartbreaking song. How awful, lonely, and self-centered this guy's life has been, and that's what he's clinging to in his final moments." But if the popularity of the song is any indication, I'm apparently in the minority in seeing it that way. Instead, it seems that people generally take satisfaction and inspiration from the ideas espoused in the song. Trying everything there is to try; having no regrets, or at least "too few to mention;" doing what you had to do, without exemption; all so you can do life on your own terms. I mean, honestly, that line of having few regrets because, after all, I only "did what I had to do, and saw it through without exemption," sounds to me just like a mobster trying to justify murder. But hey, whatever the cost, right? Just so long as he was being true to himself and doing things his way.

When we get down to it, this obviously didn't start with Frank Sinatra — the song wouldn't appeal to anyone if he was the only one who felt that way. It didn't start with #bosslife or William Randolph Hearst or Ponzi or Machiavelli or the Borgias. Our desire to be in control, to make the rules, to do things "my way" goes all the way back to the beginning. Look at Adam and Eve in the Garden. God only asked one thing of them, one thing for their own good: "Don't eat the fruit of that tree." But more than wanting to love, honor, and obey God, more than wanting paradise, more than wanting life everlasting, they wanted to be in control. So they took it and ate it. Heck (or perhaps this would be an appropriate occasion to say "Hell"), look at Lucifer himself, whose pride is best expressed in Milton's words: "Better to rule in hell than serve in heaven." I remember in one of my first acting classes here in Los Angeles, our coach explained to us students that when seeking to understand our characters' motivation, we mustn't settle for "control," since it's too universal a desire.

It couldn't help us deepen and differentiate a character simply because everybody experiences it.

This desire for control is obviously nothing new and, it would seem, it's something we all experience or relate to. So what's the problem? Well, the biggest problem is that it's not in concert with reality. While we do have free will and can control our own actions, that's not where this desire stops. We want to control circumstances and other people's actions too. It bears repeating here that if we are infringing on the free will of others unjustly, if we are using people as a means to our own ends, we're acting totally contrary to their good, to authentic love, and to their dignity as human persons. We're treating others as less than human, which isn't good for our own souls or mental well-being either. And controlling circumstances? We tend to think that if we could only control outside circumstances, we could be happy. In fact, our happiness is actually determined by what we decide to do under circumstances we can't control. As Thomas à Kempis says, "Circumstances do not make a man, but rather reveal who he is." Or, if you like, don't take my word or Thomas à Kempis's word for it. Take Gandalf's! You may remember in the film version of *The Fellowship of the Ring* that Frodo says, "I wish the Ring had never come to me. I wish none of this had happened." Gandalf replies: "So do all who live to see such times, but that is not for them to decide. All we have to decide is what to do with the time that is given us."

Underneath our desire for control is a deep fear: a fear of things going wrong, a fear of loss, a fear of pain, a fear of death. We're afraid that the only alternative to being in control is becoming a helpless victim of others and of circumstance. Now, you certainly meet people who act as though everything is out of their control, as though everything happens to them and it's all awful. "Oh how different my life would be if only XYZ didn't happen, so-and-so-and-everyone didn't treat me so poorly, and I had control of my life, but I don't." In trying to combat this defeatist victim mentality (which messes up our hearts and heads), Grant Cardone, the *10x Rule* guy I mentioned earlier, advocates going super far the other direction. He says that not only is everything in your control, you influence everything, for good or for bad. He says that if he gets into a car accident (even one where the other person is technically 100 percent "at fault") he could have left earlier in the day, given himself more time, been more alert ... he's not off the hook. Or if there's an utter apocalypse and his family isn't prepared for every single possibility, then he's the one responsible for that. Now his point here is that if we blame others and outside circumstance for everything in our lives, we're not helping ourselves. But he pushes too far in the other direction. The pendulum swings from being a victim to being a little bit of a megalomaniac ... or some other neurosis. Because, come on, while leaving earlier in the day *might* help you avoid a car accident, you have literally no way of knowing that! Some car accidents are entirely outside of your ability to influence; as are plenty of other things too. It takes humility to admit that some things are out of our control, and humility to admit that plenty of life mistakes are very much under our control. The fact is, if we buy into either a victim mentality or an "I control everything" mentality, we're forgetting entirely our relationship with God. We're latching onto fear instead of trusting in his love. But more than anything else in Scripture, God tries to remind us to trust in him, in his love for us, and in his desire for what's best for us. God says, "Be not afraid," and other iterations thereof, almost four hundred times in the Bible. A couple of other notable passages:

- "For I know the plans I have for you, says the LORD, plans for welfare and not for evil, to give you a future and a hope. Then you will call upon me and come and pray to me, and I will hear you. You seek

> me and find me; when you seek me with all your
> heart, I will be found by you, says the LORD." (Jer
> 29:11–14)

- "I came that they may have life, and have it abundantly." (Jn 10:10)
- "Fear not, for I am with you, be not dismayed, for I am your God; I will strengthen you, I will help you, I will uphold you with my victorious right hand." (Is 41:10)

So you see, this isn't a call to passively let things happen to us and be victims of circumstance, but a call to engage the world and to uphold the dignity of every person around us no matter the circumstance. This isn't a call to blame or to seek to take blame, but a call to accept responsibility for all our actions and never to pass blame in the first place. This isn't a call to control others or be controlled by others, but a call to lead out of love for others. This isn't a call to work for money and power, but a call to seek the imperishable reward of the beatific vision.

I'm writing this while we're on lockdown for the COVID-19 pandemic. For most of us, I think it's become abundantly clear during this time that, in some things, we are most definitely not in control and there's nothing we can do about it. But we don't have to be afraid. We don't have to be victims here. I don't know where my next paycheck is coming from. I don't know what I would do if my family got devastated by the virus. I can't make the entire economy go back to normal. I can't even make my friends and neighbors stay at home and respect the lockdown in hopes that it can end sooner. I can't make governments respect what they said the lockdown was for — to flatten the curve — rather than continue imposing restrictions to whatever length they deem necessary. But I can exercise my free will, not to control my circumstances or others, but to seek God, who is waiting for me. I can call upon him, come and pray to him, and do what he asks. I can fulfill the duties of my state in life to the best of my ability, blaming nothing on the circumstances, but also not living under any illusions. I can pray for my intentions, but pray more that God conform my will to his — "Thy will, not mine, be done." I can trust in him, believe he desires my greatest good, and pray "I believe, help my unbelief!" (Mk 9:24). You see, the opposite of control isn't lack of control or victimhood. It's trust. We don't need to control all the things in this life, we needn't be anxious about many things, because there is need of only one thing: to know, love, and serve God in this life, so as to enjoy happiness with him in the next.

In the end, that's the one thing we really do have control over: how we respond to the call of the God who loves us.

SO NOW WHAT?

- Take control of everything in your life. Everything. Even the things you have no possibility of changing. Own them. They're your fault and your success. Take it, it's yours!
- Or, if you'd rather introduce a little sanity into your life, start here. Which of your shortcomings do you have control over, and what can you do to change them? Hint: It usually follows a process like this: Accept and offer up the suffering you're experiencing, pray about it, take action to change.
- Where are you trying to bend things that you have no control over to your will? How can you offer those to God in trust and humility?
- Whatever happens, how can you, like St. Thomas More, see God's will in it, and how can you pray, like Jesus, "Thy will be done?"

Epilogue
Live in the Joy and Love of Christ!

(This one is actually the real title)

Hey, check it out! You're at the end of the book. *Ite missa est,* as they say. This is not a Mass, Mass is way better. But the same admonition applies. In the English translation of the Mass, the priest (or deacon) says, "The Mass is ended, go in peace," and we respond, "Thanks be to God!" which I've always thought was interesting. Are we like, "Oh thank God, FINALLY! That was so forever-taking"? While that's what it frequently sounds like to my ears, I heard a priest once explaining that, etymologically, the Latin word for Mass means something more along the lines of, "It is finished, you are dismissed." Some people have said that this dismissal hearkens to Christ's words on the cross, "It is finished," and reminds us of the saving work that we have been present to, and our call to participate in the salvation of the world. In *Sacramentum Caritatis,* Pope Benedict XVI said that for the Christian, the idea of dismissal takes on the deeper meaning of a mission:

We are dismissed for a purpose.

Through the grace of God we know our purpose, and we know that we need to live it out in love for him, and in love for neighbor as ourselves. Our mission, should we choose to accept it, is for the sake of every person in the world, and so it is necessarily a mission not of this world. G. K. Chesterton puts it this way, "We do not really want a religion that is right where we are right. What we want is a religion that is right where we are wrong. We do not want, as the newspapers say, a church that will move with the world. We want a church that will move the world." And isn't that where we started all of this? We have this instinct that our lives *mean* something. We have this yearning to fulfill the purpose that we feel, this drive to change the world. You can't change the world if you're always changing *with* the world. You must come from a place, from a spirit, that is unchanging: unchangingly good, true, and beautiful. Thanks be to God, that is where you come from! You are made in the image and likeness of the eternal God, who is truth, beauty, goodness, and love itself. You just have to become who you are.

Today you will decide whether to take orders from the world or from God; to work toward your purpose or against it. You can either accept and say yes to the fleeting pleasures and hollow accomplishments the world offers, or accept and say yes to the lasting joys and great good that God offers. You choose to whom you'll listen.

For many years I listened to the world: "The Church wants to restrict your freedom! They want to restrict your love! They want to control your life and take your money!" Sometimes I still listen to the world. But if I take a moment to think about it, I soon realize that I've spent a lot more money on things I didn't need and ended up not really wanting than I've ever given to the Church. I've suffered pain and frustration trying to follow the world's recipe for a self-centered imitation of love, and only found satisfaction in making a gift of myself. I've regretted and felt worse about myself every time I take freedom as the world defines it, the license of "doing what I want, and doing it my way," and only experienced a sense of real freedom in living from a place of deeper truth that far supersedes my own.

So perhaps, we ought to stop listening to what the world whispers in our ear about the Church's teachings. Perhaps it would be better if we heard the Church speak for herself. Then in the Church's teachings, we might hear the still, small voice of God saying, "These things I have spoken to you, that my joy may be in you, and that your joy may be full" (Jn 15:11).

About the Author

Kaiser Johnson is an actor (*Unplanned, Stranger Things*), voice-over artist (*Transformers: War for Cybertron, Call of Duty: Black Ops Cold War, Resident Evil Resistance*), and author (*Grit and Glory: Cross Training Your Body and Soul,* and an upcoming pulp adventure series). To learn more and keep up to date on his work, visit and subscribe for free at Kaiser-Johnson.com or find him @kaiserjohnson on social media.

If you loved this book, please leave a review on Amazon to help others stop being miserable and alone and instead discover a life that matters!